Final Letters

From the Yad Vashem Archive

final letters

From Victims of the Holocaust

Selected by Reuven Dafni and Yehudit Kleiman

Foreword by Chaim Herzog

President of the State of Israel

PARAGON HOUSE

NEW YORK

First American edition, 1991

Published in the United States by
Paragon House
90 Fifth Avenue
New York, NY 10011

Copyright © 1991 by Yad Vashem, Jerusalem

Originally published in Great Britain by George Weidenfeld & Nicolson Limited in 1991.

Manufactured in the United States of America
10   9   8   7   6   5   4   3   2   1

Library of Congress Cataloging-in-Publication Data
Final letters : from victims of the Holocaust / selected by Reuven Dafni & Yehudit Kleiman ; foreword by Chaim Herzog. — 1st American ed.
        p.   cm.
ISBN 1-55778-495-7 : $15.95
1. Holocaust, Jewish (1939–1945)—Personal narratives.   2. Jews—Correspondence.   I. Dafni, Reuven.   II. Kleiman, Yehudit.
D804.3.F56   1991
940.53'18—dc20   91-12984
CIP

Contents

Foreword

by Chaim Herzog, President of the State of Israel

Amongst the enormous body of literature generated by the Holocaust I am sure that this collection of letters will find a special place.

Many of them were written in the clear knowledge that their authors faced certain death; others show the hope, mixed with dreadful uncertainty and premonition, which characterized the circumstances of European Jewry in the face of the Nazi onslaught. Some record data – names, events – for coming generations; others are deeply personal messages to family and friends. Some are philosophical; others almost mundane. All show dignity and courage.

However, in reading this remarkable collection, I was struck by the clear distinction that many of the writers make between their personal fate, including the fate of their families and companions, and the collective fate of the Jewish people. Even where the authors admit that their own fate is hopeless, many of them lay on their descendants and on future generations the responsibilities of carrying out a range of tasks, some individual, some collective. In this, all display unhesitating faith in the future of the Jewish people. And history proved them right. Many of those who survived and many of their children came to join the successful struggle to establish the Jewish State immediately after the war. Indeed, some of the letters are addressed to relatives who had already escaped from Europe to what was then Palestine.

We glimpse through this material a unique picture of a series of individuals at critical and tragic points in the process of the persecution of European Jewry by the Nazis. In doing so, we all of us, more than forty years later, become part of the circle of family and friends to whom these letters are addressed. In that way it may be said that every one of these messages not only survived the Holocaust, but actually reached their destination. This may be thought to be some measure of consolation for the victims – if, indeed, consolation can exist in the face of the terrible experiences they all underwent.

In commending Yad Vashem for initiating the publication of this volume, I am particularly moved that included in it are the two letters written by my own cousin, Hanna-Hélène Goldberg, who was caught trying to escape from Paris into Vichy France in 1942 and subsequently perished in Auschwitz. It was my honour to deposit these letters in Yad Vashem, where they, too, form part of the collective memory of our people.

Chaim Herzog
Jerusalem

Introduction

by Reuven Dafni

The Yad Vashem Archives possess a collection of hundred of letters and postcards which were written by Jews under Nazi oppression. Today these missives represent a striking testimony on the Nazis' terror regime and the Jews' predicament in those conditions.

There are several characteristic features to these letters. Most of them are the last ones – final farewells, last signs of life. The inmates of camps, ghettos and prisons tried – on their way to the slaughter – to transmit to their relatives and friends some information about their fate and that of the communities; they wrote on whatever scraps of paper were at hand. Many of these messages were left in hiding places. The authors often used code words and allusions to deceive the Nazi censors. Several were dropped without envelopes from deportation trains, the authors being unaware of the destination to which they were being transported. Others were sent by regular mail or by messengers; in some cases, decades passed before they reached their destination.

Many people wrote a 'last will' when they felt that their end was near, hoping that after liberation somebody would find it and bring about its execution.

The authors were ordinary, unknown people, not destined for fame and celebrity. Most of them wrote in a personal style and sometimes used very primitive language. They sought to convey to the outside world a desperate cry of protest against their predicament and tragic fate.

We learn from these letters what people felt facing death; nevertheless, some of them are not devoid of flickers of hope and optimism: perhaps, after all . . .

We are grateful to the relatives and friends of the authors, who agreed to part with the last letters of their nearest ones and to transmit them to Yad Vashem so that they may serve as a memorial.

Letters and Postcards

When, in 1944, the Nazi rulers became increasingly aware that the powerful Third Reich was disintegrating, they began to pay attention to world opinion. Steps were taken to obfuscate the traces of German crimes. In order to camouflage the true destination of transports of Hungarian Jews who were sent to Auschwitz in the summer of 1944, the new inmates were ordered, when sending short messages to their families, to write 'Waldsee' as the sender's address – a place which did not exist.

Odon Lusztig and his two young sons, Oliver and Tibor, arrived in Auschwitz ('Waldsee') from Transylvania. Odon perished, but both boys survived. At present, Oliver is a colonel in the Romanian army and his brother lives in Israel.

8 July 1944

My dear Brother!

I am well. You also must take care of your health.

I kiss you
Oliver

ADDRESS: Lusztig Tibor
110/66 I.lego
Nagyvarad
Hungary

SENDER: Lusztig Oliver
Am Waldsee

BORN: 26.VII.1928

I have arrived safely. I am well and in good spirits. Everything is fine with me.

Best regards
Odon Lusztig

ADDRESS: Lapusan Janos
          g.kath. lelkesz
          Solyomko
          Kolozs megye
          Hungary
SENDER: Lusztig Odon
          Am Waldsee
BORN: 24.VI.1899

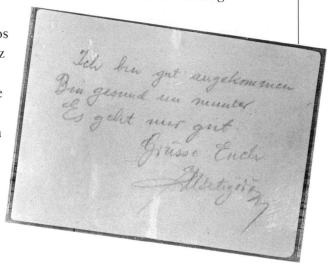

The ship *Mefkure* left Romania for Israel on 3 August 1944 with about 430 survivors of the Holocaust on board. On 20 August the ship was torpedoed by a German warship and most of the passengers perished.

Rica was seventeen years old when she died.

2 August 1944

Dearest Mama,

I am writing this in Constanta and in a short while we shall get on the boat.

Rica

This is my second letter to you. In front of me there is the sea and it is entrancing – beautiful. What can I write at this time?! I am happy and full of expectations and curiosity for my future.

I am kissing you and I am looking forward to our reunion in the near future.

Warm greetings to all the family and friends,

Rica

In May 1944 Lia Goldstein, who lived in a small town in Transylvania, Hungary, sent three letters to her husband Ferenc, who was in a forced labour camp. The woman and her child, four-year-old Theodor (Teddy), were deported to Auschwitz, where they perished. Mr Goldstein (today Meir Amrami) survived and lives with his family in Israel.

2.5.1944

My dearest,

I have just heard that they are accepting parcels only today – so I am putting this together in a great hurry. Don't be angry that I am sending torn socks. I hope that you received the parcel which I sent with mended ones and also two pairs of new socks and underpants. I am in despair. Some say that the 'visitors' will arrive this evening, but others deny this. I am in a bad mood, perhaps everything will still turn out for the best and I have worried for no reason. The Almighty knows what will be. Let's hope that no harm will befall us.

Many kisses,
Lia and Teddy

Lia and Teddy Goldstein

My Dearest,   3.5.1944

We are leaving today. I took food for 20 days. I had caramel cake,
toast, beans, etc.
    Keep well, may the good Lord guard you.

Many kisses,
Lia and Teddy

My Dearest,   3.5.1944

We are leaving now. Don't take it to heart, we are together with all
the village. You must accept the fact that we too are no exception.
We are well provided for. We are going by train. They are not
accepting parcels now, only in 10 days' time – then we'll send you
a parcel with tobacco, felt pants, etc. I hope you'll also receive
money.

Don't worry, don't torment yourself. Teddy is impatient for us to leave. They have assembled us in the courtyard of Moissi; from here we'll go to the railway station. Pray.

Kisses,
Lia and Teddy

Ida Goldis of Romania was deported with her young son, Vili, and her sister, Doba, to Transnistria in November 1941. The deportees had to make the journey on foot, and Ida carried Vili on her back. In the severe cold the child froze to death. His mother died soon afterwards of an intestinal infection caused by polluted water; she was twenty-two.

The letter presented below was the last one Ida was able to write and send via a messenger to her eldest sister, Clara, who had stayed in Romania. Both sisters, Clara and Doba, survived the war and kept the letter until Doba's daughter, Yehudit Sheli, who lives in Israel, transmitted it to Yad Vashem, where she works.

4 November 1941

Dear Clara,

Yesterday I sent you a postcard which, if you receive it, will cause you a great deal of sorrow. I am writing to you now thanks to the goodwill of this gentleman, and I beg you not to tell Mother the truth, since it is too awful and I do not want this matter to impair her health, which is poor anyway. My dear sister, for a few days a terrible danger has been threatening us, we shall be sent on foot to the Ukraine (so they tell us) for colonization there. You can imagine our situation when we must go such a long way on foot, the weather being so cold, with a small child and with the few things which we

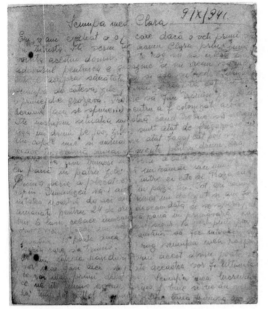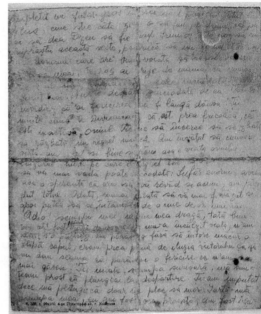

will be able to drag along, that is to say, only food for the journey. They say that we shall be sent in groups of 2,500 persons, so that within four days nobody will remain here. The first group left yesterday, among them Rosa with the children, may God protect them. Yesterday our Committee here sent a representative [to the authorities], so they postponed our departure for twenty-four hours, for the time being, and there is hope that it will be postponed for another six months, that means, until spring. At six o'clock we will receive the final answer, and you can imagine our panicky state of mind. Perhaps, as a result of this extension, even the group which has already left will return. I am asking you, my dear sister, to answer me through this gentleman. Perhaps he will still find us here, and maybe these will be the last words I will receive from you. My darling, the things and the money which you have sent me helped me greatly and arrived at the proper time. From the wool that you

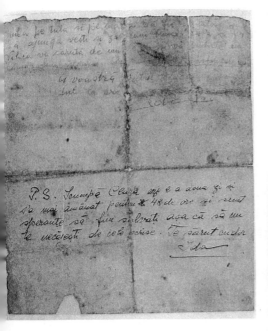

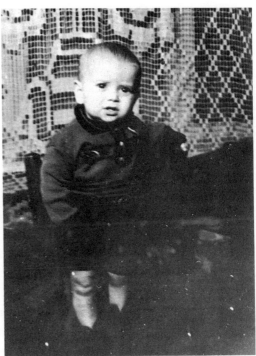

Vili Goldis

have sent me I have made a thick shawl for Vili's neck, because who knows how many days we will be on the way; at least, may God give us fine weather. I beg you not to spread this news in order not to bring any harm to this man of goodwill. My dear, please care for Mother, since you will be the only remaining member of her family. Never do what we have done, never separate from her. How much I envy you the luck to be with her. You remember how I used to scold you for being cowardly, for not being active enough, claiming that one must try to fight for one's existence. I do not regret anything, such is human life. The only thing I regret is that my eyes will not see you any more. I am suffering so much. I hoped that we would see each other again, but now I have lost everything, all hope. Once, only once to have the chance to meet you again, and then – may the worst come.

Goodbye, my dear ones! My beloved Mother, my good Father,

you were the first sunshine which warmed my life. I did not know how to preserve this warmth, I left without so much as casting a glance backward. I was too full of illusions about the future to be able to understand that I was abandoning a happiness which I would never recover. You remember, my dear sister, how embarrassed I felt when you wept at our leave-taking, and how angry I was with you because of your tears, since I (so I thought) was not going to die after all. Forgive me, my dear, it was I who was the fool. I was light-headed, I believed that one could catch every appealing thing that came in sight. I probably was too young. But what's the use of apologizing? I regret from the very depth of my soul that, on departing, I did not realize the importance of the moment, that I did not take a long, long look at you, so that your image would remain deeply engraved in my soul like an icon, that I did not hug you tightly, never releasing you from my arms. Now I am looking back in vain, it is hopeless, since fate has struck a cruel blow at our lives; I may try ever so hard to get nearer to you, and yet we are being dragged away relentlessly, farther and farther. I want so much to be together with you (after all, we did succeed in becoming close again), to rest at your feet, tired from so much hardship, to find peace there and to leave you never more. Often I lay awake at night and imagined the moment when I would meet you again; I drugged myself with these thoughts and enjoyed endlessly that waking dream.

Now I have no hopes left, God did not want us to meet again. I suppose that I have sinned too much. Goodbye, my darling sister, good luck to you, bring up your dear children in happiness and good health. Thousands of kisses on your sweet eyes. Does Revelina still remember me? May it be God's will that you soon see Carol again and that you live happily without worries and sufferings. Kisses to Father and Mother, may they live in good health and enjoy better news. Doba and Vili send you thousands of kisses and a fond farewell.

Clara, answer me please.

Goodbye forever, all my thoughts are with you.

Ida

p.s. Clara darling, for the second time within the last two days our departure has been postponed for twenty-four hours, so that there is some hope for us to be saved. So do not worry because of what I have written.

Kisses
Ida

Both the letter and the postcard below were written by the Dutch Jewish Knoop sisters, Hein and Wim, in Amsterdam to Mr van Zijl, a resident of the same city. The letter was dispatched before the sisters' transfer to the Westerbork camp; the card, dropped from the deportation train, also reached its destination.

Tuesday

Dear boys,

We were very happy with your package, it was wonderful, the cake in particular was very delicious. We are sitting in a train, 40 of us in a freight wagon. Mama and Papa are also with us. Nany is in the S. waggon. We received your package last night. Thank you so much for the wonderful care you bestow upon us. Hopefully we will see each other soon. Call Delome, give regards to him and to all our friends. We think of you a lot. We are probably going to Riga, that's where mother is also. Some are in W[esterbork]. It could be difficult there. Within 3 days we were already filthy. The

spirit is great, we did not shed a tear. We are just completely numb.
Regards to Roel, Lex, Leo, Joke and for you a hearty kiss.

Hein

ADDED IN A DIFFERENT HANDWRITING:
Dear boys, Also my best wishes. We all hope that soon we will be
on our way back. We shall try to survive. Regards, *Wim*.

* * *

It is Saturday afternoon and we still don't know anything. We hope
for the best. I am coming back, that is for sure, count on it. I feel
very strong and I can definitely survive. Yesterday, Friday, I received
a package, it was wonderful. Find out from Schouwburg [transit
centre for deportations in Amsterdam] whether we are still there.
In case we are not yet deported, please send me a pan, because I
have no pan to eat from when the food is distributed. Dear
sweethearts, think about 108 that should not be forgotten. I have
plenty of news. Take care of yourselves and your dear child. Dear
children, I think much about you all. We have gone through so
much happiness and sorrow, that I will never forget, neither will

you. Just make sure to prepare a delicious cup of coffee when I come home.

Bye, Leontje, Lex and Roel, may God spare you.

Thousand kisses,
Mother, Esther

P.S. Sunday. Just received your 2 beautiful packages. Dear Leontje, Roel, Lex and Gen and baby, if we don't return – here are last regards from the heart.

- - -

On the eve of the liquidation of the Jews in the small town of Moletai in Lithuania, Zipora, a young woman, wrote her farewell letter to her husband in South Africa. It was probably thrown out of the building where all the Jews were assembled prior to the action. A Lithuanian woman found the letter and kept it until she was able to give it to a relative of the family, who visited the Soviet Union some twenty years later, in the 1960s. Meanwhile, Zipora's husband had died.

Dear Moshe Bune Bayle,

May you all remain in good health and we will be good pleaders [with God, in the next world] for you. The man who will send you this letter is to be paid. We have been fasting for two days now and we are going to the slaughter. Our *Yohrzeit** will be 29 August, so observe it. Father is not at home and, who knows, he must be gone for a long time by now. We are standing dressed up, all of us, with my dear little children and are waiting. We are all in the *beth-hamidrash*† now and have had enough of this life, so that many a time one wished death to come. Already on the eve of Rosh Hodesh Av‡, they lined us up to be shot, but a miracle happened, and today our miracle would be if God has mercy on us. Only if we are shot will he [the man] send you the letter. Moshe, they are after your little kids, that is what they want. So goodbye and keep strong. We Jews are sacrificing ourselves for your redemption.

Zipora

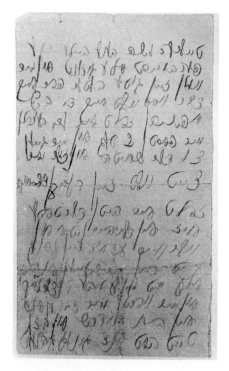

ADDRESS IN ENGLISH:
Mr B. Buck,
P.O. Alberton,
T.v.l. [Transvaal], South Africa

* The day on which Jews commemorate the death of a family member by lighting a candle.

† A school for teaching the Torah, usually within the premises of a synagogue.

‡ The first day of the new month of the Hebrew calendar; the month of Av is July or August depending on the year.

3 June 1942

My dear ones!

I am looking for an occasion to send you this letter indirectly, so as to be able to inform you about our desperate situation. In general, you do know what our position is in our native country, but you cannot possibly imagine the immense tragedy which is taking place here. Tens of thousands of our fellow nationals have already left the country almost barefoot and naked. Now our turn has come. By the 14th of this month we are due to leave our present locality, as all Jewish inhabitants of the small communities are obliged to gather in the district towns of their regions, from where they are being sent away in transports. In sealed cattle cars, of course. What is their destination? They disappear! I hope that I will be able to bear the hardship which we will have to face. Old people and babies, and even the disabled and severely ill persons will be sent for liquidation in this 'humane Christian' manner (words of the officer in charge here).

Well, God Almighty might still help us at the last moment. Our only hope is for such a 'miracle', but unfortunately it has no intention of occurring.

Many of our comrades in distress save their lives by escaping to you. Unfortunately, this way out is barred for us. You do know what happened to dear Jeno! He was forced to give up his business and apartment. His Ilse was deported to Poland this year on 27 March along with thousands of other young girls and single women aged 16–45. None of them can send any message to their families.

25

Jeno and Egon reported voluntarily to the labour camp in [name erased]. Jeno wrote me once from there. Egon works as a carpenter, a profession which he learned in a slap-dash manner when he had to shift to another job, and Jeno is employed as a sanitary officer. He wrote on a censored postcard that they were doing well, but they did not know how long they would be able to stay there.

Concerning me and my wife, we really have been doing very well since we arrived here, we have fully recovered, and we hope therefore that God Almighty will protect us in future as well by giving us the strength and the courage to endure all this.

From our children in Eretz [Israel] we have received no message since November, and since May of last year no news has arrived from our youngest son either. Please write to Kefar Hamaccabi, Haifa, P.O.B. 1453. Have you by any chance had a letter from Abi? Please write through the International Red Cross. Why can't you answer our previous letter? – Goodbye, then! I will try to write to you once again.

Many warm kisses from your devoted
[*signature illegible*]

3. VI. 1942. –

Meine Lieben!

Burgkunstadt
24 April 1942
4 o'clock in the morning

My dear Elisabeth,

Only now have I finished and can lie down for a while. No chance for a sleep today, though. So I use these few free minutes to say goodbye to you once more.

I will always remember those joyful and beautiful hours which I spent in your home and which helped me to surmount the hardships of that time.

Will I see you again? After all, we are both still young and you never know. It is a consolation that this is not one person's fate, but that of many thousands.

I wish you, dear Elisabeth, as well as your dear parents, best luck. With affectionate greetings,

Always devoted to you,
Eva

When writing to your grandparents, please send them my kindest regards.

Below is an exchange of brief, censored correspondence between Alfred Neumann, a prisoner in the Buchenwald camp, and his wife.

---

17 November 1938

Dear Lili,

Everything is fine with me. I am well, hopefully you and Mother are too.

Many regards and kisses from your loving husband [the last word is crossed out]
Alfred

STAMP: Mail Censorship Office

ADDRESS: Mrs Lili Neumann,
           Breslau,
           78 Goethe St.

SENDER: Alfred Neumann,
           No. 27258,
           Block Ia,
           Concentration Camp Buchenwald,
           Post office Weimar/Thuringen

Breslau 25 November 1938

My beloved Fredy,

Just now I have received your kind card and I am glad that you are well. We are fine, too. I am liquidating the household and we are moving to Taschen Street. I have sent you 15 marks so that you can

Breslau,   den 25.11.38.

Mein geliebter Fredy! Soeben erhalte ich Deine liebe
Karte und ich freue mich, dass Du gesund bist. Uns
geht es auch gut, ich löse den Haushalt auf und wir
ziehen auf die Taschenstr. Ich sandte Dir 15 Mark,
damit Du Dir Zigaretten kaufen kannst oder was Du
sonst brauchst. Halte Dich tapfer und denke immer
daran, dass ich in Gedanken jede Minute bei Dir bin.
Ich küsse Dich vielmals in Liebe   Deine *Lili*.

Auch von mir herzliche Grüße
Mutter

Abs. Lili Neumann
Breslau
Goethestr. 78.

Postkarte

Zurück

6

Deutsches Reich

26.11.38

Adressat hat bis auf weiteres Postsperre!

an den Schutzhäftling

Alfred Neumann

Nr. 27 258 Block Ia

N...   258   Block Ia

Konzentrationslager
Buchenwald

Post Weimar /Thür.

Straße, Hausnummer,
Gebäudeteil, Stockwerk

5436

buy cigarettes or whatever else you need. Be brave and always remember that in my mind I am with you every minute.

many, many kisses,
Your loving *Lili*

From me, too, affectionate regards   *Mother*

ADDRESS: Security Prisoner Alfred Neumann,
            No. 27258,
            Block Ia,
            Concentration Camp Buchenwald,
            Post office Weimar/Thuringen

SENDER: Lili Neumann,
            Breslau,
            78 Goethe St.

STAMP: Returned. The addressee is under a post ban until further notice.

On the eve of the deportation of the Belgrade Jews, Regina Kandt entrusted her Christian neighbour with a letter to her husband and children. Faithful to her promise, the neighbour kept the letter and transmitted it after the war to Regina's relatives in Israel, through the agency of the Israeli Embassy in Belgrade.

One of Regina's children, a son to whom she refers in the letter as 'Milček', today lives in Israel under the name of Reuven Dafni. He belonged to a group of parachutists from Palestine who were dropped into Yugoslavia in the spring of 1944 with the mission of rescuing Jews behind the German frontlines.

In November 1941, close to 10,000 women and children from Belgrade and other areas were assembled at a place called Sajmište, near the town of Zemun, and murdered there.

My dearest Maks,

Today or tomorrow I shall be taken to the camp, may God help me to overcome this too. I suffered greatly, but I stood it because I believe in the good God and because my great love for you, Mutzek, kept me going. Already for months I have not heard anything from both of you. Jaza and Katjusha know everything. I stacked away a little bit so that, if our good God will give us the good fortune of seeing one another again, not everything will be lost. Katjusha was wonderful. Everything is being arranged according to the possibilities. Sasha and Eva are coming with me, but I do not know how long we shall stay together. I sent you, through Jasa, 10,000 Italian lira; hopefully you received them. Mutzek, I greatly loved

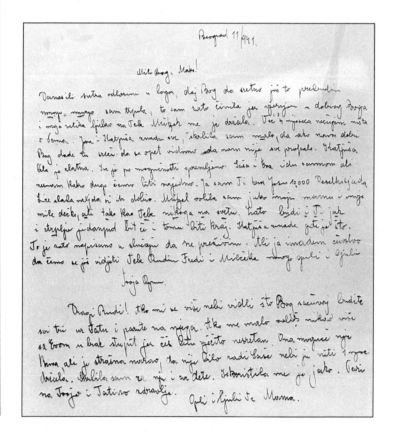

my mother and my dear boys, but I did not love anybody in the whole world as much as I loved you. Therefore you too must be strong and patient, sometime there will be an end to this too. Katjusha knows where everything is. I am writing this only in the eventuality that I shall not survive. But I do have the feeling that we shall see one another again.

You, Rudi, Fredi and Milček embraces and love,

your *Regina*

* * *

Dear Rudi,

In case we shall not see one another ever again, God forbid, all three of you must be with father and take care of him. If you love me even a little bit, do not remarry Eva because you will be eternally unhappy. It may not be her fault, but she has a terrible character. If it had not been for little Sasha, I might not have kept her. I slaved for her and for the child. She exploited me greatly. Take care of your and of father's health.

Love and embraces,
Mother

Hanna-Hélène Goldberg of Paris was caught while trying to cross the border in her attempt to escape to Vichy France in 1942. She was deported to the camps of Drancy and Poitiers, from where she wrote to her mother in Paris. Drancy and Poitiers were transit camps for Jews deported from France to death-camps, mainly to Auschwitz. The letters were written in French. Her last letter, written on the way to Auschwitz, was probably dropped from the train.

The letters were transmitted to Yad Vashem by Hanna's cousin, Mr Chaim Herzog, President of the State of Israel.

Tuesday, 18 August 1942

My dear Maman,

I received your letter this morning and it worried me very much because of the matter of the furniture. If you must pay 1,000 francs monthly out of what you receive, this is going to be very difficult. I suppose that you have had no news from Isi, as you do not mention this, and, on the other hand, according to what you have told me about Lea (here, there is also much talk about this), I am afraid there could be difficulties in receiving news from Isi in the future.

My dear Maman, you must not be sad, you must not lose courage. I, for one, am not afraid of what will happen to me, because I am sure I will get out of this, and then I don't think that it will last for more than a few months, and I probably will not be deported. I repeat to you: what makes me feel miserable is the certitude that you are more unhappy there at home than I ever will be in the worst conditions – because I am in the middle of it, so I can react, while you are suffering for me and you can do nothing except think of me. I do not want you to despair all day long, to get exhausted, to get ill. You must be confident. I am strong enough to endure what happens to me, the more so as I will surely be released soon and join you again in a few months. Do hope. You cannot imagine how sad I feel when I read certain things that you recount to me, like how you did not want to change your dress, etc. As for me, when I think of you, I see you in that blue dress which you had made not long ago, with that collar, pocket and belt, with a good hair-do, fresh, as you look when you pay a little attention to yourself, and I fear to find you different when I come back. Look, so many people have gone away, and yet they have come back. If I were a boy, I would have gone to fight in the war, which would have been much worse. Here nothing bad can happen to me. I will return soon, and we will trace Rosette, and we will go to see Dadoun, and everything will be fine, and we will be happy again.

But when I imagine that you are crying, that you are sad the whole day – this hurts me so much, more than all that might happen to me. Thus, Maman, I would like you to make an effort, to bear in mind that I am young, in good health, that I will get myself out of this, and that everything will turn out well after all.

I do not need a spirit-stove here, as there is wood to be found around, and, if someone wants to cook something, there is a stove in each room. What's more, if I am later in Drancy, there are limitations as to the weight of the parcels, and I would not be able to get any spirit [there], let alone the fact that spirit is not available anywhere.

As to the parcels: I do not know exactly when we are going to leave here, so should you dispatch a parcel to me, and should it arrive after my departure (you will know if this happens, because on the day of our departure I will send you a postcard, which will mean that I have not received anything), please write immediately to the camp and ask them to return it. Presumably, when there is a request to return a package to the sender, they comply.

Tell Na's mother that all those who belonged to her group have experienced the same fate. As to the packages, send what you can. I already have eaten the first and have not yet received the second. I will see tomorrow or Thursday if something arrives.

You have done well in snubbing Mrs Kn., she really considers us to be idiots. Now perhaps she will understand.

It is no use pondering over the problem of why or how things happened. This is a question of luck or rather bad luck, that is all. Do not send me any bread, better send biscuits, which keep longer.

There are a gentleman and a lady here, Alsatians, about sixty years old, very fine people whose family name is Herzog. I have talked with them and they were delighted – he told me that he was not a relative of ours, but was slightly acquainted with Grandfather. They live near Ternes. He is Rabbi Metzger's cousin.

There is also a Mrs Lew.[inski] of Joinville here. She is very nice.

I have not yet written to Rosette. I regret that you have written to her, there was no need to distress her. It is true, however, that should she remain without news about me for several months, she would worry. There is a kind of rabbi here, his name is Pomeranz and he has set up a minyan. He is not particularly nice.

I kiss you affectionately, dear Maman, and please don't worry yourself sick.

Nana

* * *

Friday 18 September [*1942*]

My dear Maman,

I left Drancy yesterday and at this moment I am in the train. We are moving in the direction of Metz, but I don't know whether we will stop there, since they say that the journey will last for three days. I have much courage. This is a bad period to go through. I am absolutely sure that I will see you again, my dear Maman, in a few months. You must stay very brave, you must not be sad. At this moment I am with friends from Poitiers. I will always manage one way or another. I think that I will not be able to write to you, but don't despair. I am always thinking of you. Don't abandon yourself to distress. My morale is very strong. I have plenty of courage and hope.

I embrace you affectionately. Too bad that your and St.'s joint efforts did not work, please transmit the news to him. I hope to see you soon, don't despair.

Nana

You must all take care of yourselves. Perhaps it would be good for you, Maman, to work at the Bienf. [aisance].

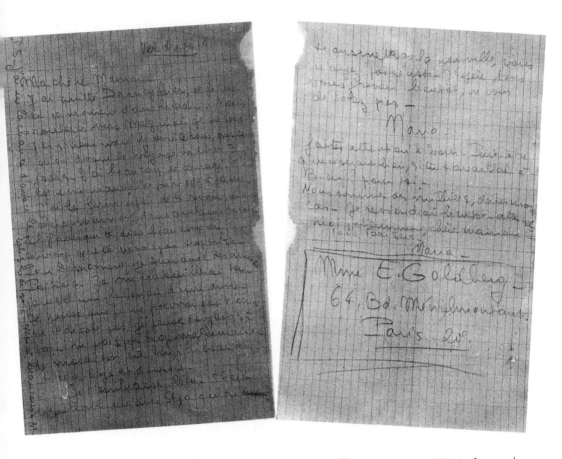

There are thousands in my situation. I will return soon. Wait for me patiently, dear Maman.

> 1,000 kisses
> *Nana*

P.S. I was lucky to receive the parcel yesterday evening. Thank you so much. N.

ADDRESSED TO: Mme E. Goldberg,
                  64, Bd. Menilmontant,
                  Paris 20-e.

The Rubin family of Vienna, father, mother and two sons, Herbert
and Max, tried desperately to emigrate from Austria after its
annexation by the Reich. They turned to their friends in the USA –
the Dushman couple – begging them for help. It is not known
whether the Rubins succeeded in escaping.

Vienna
3 November 1938

Dear Mrs Dushman,

We are extremely grateful to you for your kind letter, which we
appreciate very much. Only yesterday my son wrote you a letter in
English and today I will answer yours in German. Highly esteemed,
madam, you cannot even imagine how much good you have done
by your kind words. We were in such deep despair already that the
most awful thoughts haunted us, since we absolutely must leave
the country, and so far there has been no way out for us. Just today
we imagined the worst – and, lo and behold, your kind letter
arrived. I must admit, you are our saviour, because it is you who
have inspired us with new courage, and we cling to you like
drowning people do. I am sure that you are the only person who
can help us, and may God reward you doubly for your good deed.
We have appealed to relatives in the U.S.A. and they did send us an
affidavit; unfortunately, the American Consulate informed us that
it was not sufficiently substantial. Now I dare to ask you this great
favour – please send us [another] affidavit and contact my relatives.
Their address is: Rosa Hermann, 164 Sherman St., Passaic, New
Jersey, U.S.A.

I want to stress again that we will not be a burden to anybody,
we are all healthy and strong, and not pampered. As you are surely
very busy, I take the liberty of suggesting that you should entrust

some shipping agency with the whole matter; let them make all the arrangements, and we, in return, commit ourselves to purchase our travel tickets at this agency as well as to cover all the expenses which are due from us.

Thus, I express once more my deep gratitude for your goodwill, and beg you desperately to answer as quickly as possible.

Yours devotedly,
A. Rubin
1/12 Rafael St, Vienna 20

* * *

Vienna
20 December 1938

Dear Professor, Dear Madam,

I greatly appreciate your letter which I received today, along with the acknowledgement of the American Consulate that the affidavit issued by you has reached them by now. I take the liberty of expressing in this way, for the time being, my deep gratitude for your kindness; may God recompense you doubly for this generous deed. Believe me, we were already so deep in despair that we saw no solution. You are our saviour and we hope now that, owing to your kind assistance, the sun will shine for us again. Your comforting words gave us fresh strength and new courage. However, I permit myself to tell you about the information I received simultaneously from the American Consulate to the effect that the affidavit is not sufficiently substantial, which is the reason why the Consulate is requesting a supplementary voucher. Also a tax attestation should be enclosed. Thus, may I ask you kindly to provide the missing documents; since we absolutely must leave the country, the matter is extremely urgent for us. Please do not

Wien, 20/XII. 1938.

Sehr geehrter Herr Professor und
sehr geehrte gnädige Frau!

Heute erhielt ich Ihren werten
Brief und zugleich die Verständigung
vom amerikanischen Konsulat, dass das
von Ihnen ausgestellte Affidavit bereits
eingelangt ist. Ich erlaube mir vor-
läufig auf diesem Wege für Ihr Güte
innigst zu danken und der liebe Gott
möge Ihnen diese gute Tat doppelt
lohnen. Glauben Sie uns, unsere Ver-
zweiflung war schon so groß, dass
wir uns gar keinen Rat finden
konnten. Sie sind unsere Retter
und wir hoffen nun, dass durch

Tat beruen werden.

Nun wünsche ich Ihnen sehr
geehrter Herr und sehr geehrte
gnädige Frau das beste Wohl-
ergehen und verbleibe mit den
herzlichsten Grüßen Ihr
ewig dankbarer

Abraham Tauber Rubin

Auch von meiner Frau und
Kinder die ergebensten Grüße.

consider us as being importunate – we turn to you because we have nobody else to help us. Only you are our rescuers. I am also very grateful to you for having sent us your photograph, which I appreciate very much. I show this picture to everybody because you are our sunshine in these gloomy days. I take the liberty of sending you ours as well, and I promise you that you shall never regret your good deed.

Wishing you all the best, I remain, dear sir and dear madam, With my kindest regards,

your forever grateful,
Abraham Tauber Rubin

My wife and children also send you the expressions of their deepest devotion.

This is the last letter of Karl Treifer, which he sent from Lvov to his sister Gini in the year 1940.

Lvov 29 January 1940

My dear ones,

I have sent you already 2 postcards and a cable, and am without any news. Everyone gets mail from Romania, only I don't. I am very upset not to hear anything from you and ask you to reply immediately, either by letter or telegram, if you are well and how you are doing. I cannot write much about myself, I am so half and half, I am still suffering from the injury to my hand, of which I have told you already. How are you, my dear ones? How is Papa? And Milo, how are you, dear Klara? I hope all are healthy. What does Jenny write? Please give her my address so that she can write to me. I cannot tell you how things are here. I am very upset, I do not know how you are and ask you again to respond immediately. Tomorrow we have the memorial day for our dear unforgetable Mama. Do not think that I forget. Well, once again, please answer immediately, I send warmest kisses to all, all of you.

Yours,
Karl

P.S. Best greetings to everyone.
My address is Karl Treifer, Lvov, Post Restante.

Susel Gathel from Breslau was the daughter of a Jewish father and an Aryan mother who had converted to Judaism. According to the racial laws, Susel was a half-Jewess and was deported to a forced labour camp for *'Mischlinge'* (mixed races), where she died shortly after the liberation in an American hospital. Her brother, Itzhak, who went with Youth Aliyah (an Israeli organization which helped child emigrants) to Eretz Israel in the 1930s, enlisted as a soldier with the British Army and returned to Germany with the Allied troops. He and his mother settled in Israel.

My beloved little Mother,

I am greatly worried about you. Keep your head up. Everything is quiet here. I can hardly believe that you will ever succeed in coming here again. Do write anyhow – whatever arrives, arrives – but only unimportant matters. Whatever happens, take father's papers with

you and in particular the certificate from Auschwitz, the death
certificate.

Fondest kisses

your *Susel*

P.S. Write immediately and daily.

Mrs Hedda is here today and tells us about the terrible chaos.
Everything will be all right in the end. I don't know if it is a good
idea to send more letters by mail. Please stay well and strong.

Fondest kisses,

Susel

* * *

21 January 1945

Beloved little Mother,

Again a letter, but Mrs Hauffer will leave only tomorrow morning
and thus this one might arrive sooner. Let Mrs Fischer tell you. I
was looking out constantly today because I thought you might be
able to squeeze through. Mother, stay brave. For the time being all
seems to go quite well with us. Get yourself foodstuff. Buy
everything!! We are very quiet here and it would be the best for us
if we could be permitted to stay here. I also wish you were here
with me. You need not worry for me. Albert Hadeler and I, we
shall manage. What does the Baurat say? Convey my greetings to
all of them. Stay well, my dearest mother.

Fondest kisses,

yours

Susel

In case you come, come almost without luggage because of the
carrying.

Bialystok Ghetto 4 March 1943

Please go to my sister. Her residence is in Jerusalem. I do not
remember the address. Her present name is Shoshanah Fink. To
convey greetings. I do not know anything at all about the family.
I was still at home at the time of the Soviets. For the last time.
Today they are certainly not alive any longer. I also shall not live
any more, one more week, perhaps one more month.

I would have liked to meet her again. It's a pity. I send her
greetings.

Zippora

Budapest
16 October 1944 6.15 p.m.

My Dear Brother,

Goodbye! Think of our talk that night. I felt as one with you. I knew that, if it were you whose life would end, I would go on living as if I had lost half of my body and soul. You said that, if I die, you will kill yourself. Think of what I told you, that if you stay alive I will live on within you. I would have liked to continue my life, with you and with our family. Plans, desires, hopes were before me. I longed for the unknown. I would have liked to know, to live, to see, to do, to love. . . . But now it is all over. In the city, Jews were exterminated from entire streets. There is no escape. Tonight or at the latest tomorrow it will be our turn. At seventeen I have to face certain death. There is no escape. We thought that we would be exceptions, but fate made no exceptions. I always felt the pull of the depth, about which I have written to you. . . . I believe, I also felt, that I would die young. It seems like fate put a curse on each of us. After Jisrael [eldest brother, who died at nineteen] it is now my turn together with my father, mother and Sorele [sister]. I hope you will survive us. Farewell and forgive me if ever I have offended you. (For the first time my eyes begin to fill with tears. I am careful not to cry as there are others present.) Because I loved you and I see you as you smile, (the vein on your brow is swelling) as you are thinking, as you eat, as you smoke, as you sleep and I feel great tenderness, great love and my eyes are filled with tears. Farewell. Live happily, all the best to you my dear brother, lots of success, much love and happiness, don't weep, don't cry. (I felt so bad hearing you cry that night.) Think of me lovingly. Remember me with good heart and, if there is another world (how much I discussed it with you, too – now I'll find out! My poem 'What Will Happen to Me?' comes to my mind . . . I felt it already then), then I will pray to God to help you in whatever you do. Farewell, my dear only brother! If you are interested to know my state of mind (you see I am thinking of this, too) I will try to describe it and also that of our home.

The calamity started last evening. By nightfall, the Jews of [houses no.] 64 and 54 had already been taken away. There was a pool of blood on the pavement, but by morning it was washed away. I was awake the whole night. R.J. and K.S. [friends] were here. Poor R.J. could hardly stand on his feet he was so full of fright. At first we hoped that the police and the army would protect us, but after a phone call we learned everything. Slowly morning arrived, but the events of the day made our situation hopeless. K.S. came at 6. He was about to faint after he fought with four Nazis who beat him terribly. He barely escaped with his life. He was stumbling and trembling and could not start talking because of what he had seen and been through. I write fast, who knows if I will have time to finish? K.S. offered to take Sorele to a safe place. She promptly jumped at the suggestion and wanted to go immediately. But Mummy stepped in front of her and with a completely calm voice said that she would not let her go because the Nazis might catch them on the street. Sorele was crying and hysterical. She wanted to go, she wants to live. Finally Mother proposed that if I go too then she will give her consent. You should have heard the way she said that. Sorele wanted to go, I stayed . . . I could not leave our mother and father. (Do you remember our discussion about hiding in the safe hide of a bear? It came to my mind at once.) So mother did not let Sorele go and K.S. did not force it any longer, he, too, stayed. Sorele cried and screamed, Father was praying the whole night. He still has some hope left, but he is talking about this world as being like a vestibule to prepare ourselves to the real world to come.

Mother and Father are telling religious parables to K.S. about the inevitability of destiny. Mathild [an aunt] is sitting next to us and listens. Sorele is outside and I am writing. I am relatively calm, facing death my thoughts are coherent. (Yesterday at dawn I even wrote a steno-composition, you might find it in my notebook.) It is not fear that I feel but the terribly considered bitter and painful realization of things to come. I hope I'll get it over with quickly, only it will be terrible to see each other's agony. God will help us and we will be over it.

Farewell, dear, sweet Brother. Farewell! Remember me. I hope that I, too, will be able to think of you even from over there. I would like to hug and kiss you once more. But who knows to whom I write these lines? Are you alive?! Farewell, my dear brother, my sweet Mordchele, live happily. Kissing you for the last time – till we meet again,

Your Loving Brother

Helena Mandelbaum was born in Cracow in 1925 and held a Costa Rican passport. She was in a protected camp when the Nazis entered and sent her to Drancy in the summer of 1944. From there she was deported to Auschwitz, where she perished. Helena was an only child. The letter was written in Polish.

My dear ones,

This is my farewell letter. We are going to a concentration camp in France, to Drancy. You know already what will happen to us after this.

I *ask you urgently*: send a message via Paris to Ana and to my mother. Perhaps one can still do something for us. I have the impression that everything is all right in Titmoning. Write to father. The situation is distressing.

Perhaps a quick rescue might still help.

My dear ones, keep this letter, it is perhaps the last one and perhaps you will show it one day to my dear mother. Tell her that I was with her in my thoughts until the last moment of my life. If my father should be rescued, take care of him and see to it that he does not do, God forbid, some stupid thing.

Life without me will be unbearable for mother.

I implore you, do whatever is still possible to rescue me.

Thank you very much for everything you have done for me, most of all, thanks to mother.

I conclude because my heart bursts with pain.

Remember me and do everything via Paris.

Kisses from me,
yours,
Hela.

Doris Perlhefter and her mother were deported from Theresienstadt to Krivoklat in Bohemia and then to a forced labour camp in Estonia. They managed to send these letters, which they wrote in Reval to the German wife of a Jew, Karl (who is also mentioned in the letters), when they worked for the Holzman company with the help of a German supervisor named Max Schimkat.

Doris, who was at that time twenty-one years old and survived, handed these letters to Yad Vashem.

Please, be so kind as to transfer enclosed letter.

25 May 1942

(written from Krivoklat, Bohemia) If I may offer sound advice, do not do it, the matter via O.F., it is extremely dangerous, if you are not absolutely sure.

Dear Mrs Maria,

You will probably not believe me if I tell you how very pleased I was with your two letters, it is wonderful after such a long time to receive again a real letter from that world, and particularly if it is full of optimism, like yours. After all, we all are in an optimistic mood here, this is because of the Cz[ech] surroundings, but I do believe you a little bit more!

I am starting this letter even before I can confirm receipt of your parcel, because we have 2 days of vacation, on weekdays it is almost impossible to write, unless one plays hooky in the forest and retires for half an hour into the forest. Please be not surprised about my scribble, I am writing in bed (which is, by the way, on the first floor).

Well, let me come to the matter. I have conveyed the contents of your first letter as well as possible to K. We are permitted to write to them once weekly, but only a postcard in printed letters. To tell the truth, I do not believe that K. will get my card. First, it takes, according to the cards which they send from there to us, at least 3 weeks, and second, I fear, that the postal ban is also aimed at us. Dear Mrs Maria, could you not find out what happened there? We are terribly worried here, and there are the worst rumours, which we would rather not believe. I will try to answer all your questions as well as I can, of course much may have changed in the meantime. One is housed in various barracks which are more or less old-fashioned ones. There are altogether 3 barracks for women and 3 for men and one mixed, where old people live. 25–30 people live in one normal room, there are also halls in one barracks where 200–500 persons are housed; on the other hand we, for instance, live in a small cosy little room for 12 persons. In most of the rooms there are by now already wooden beds, 2–3 storeys high, one crawls up on a ladder, it is really very orderly, cosy, and, what is most important, one can sleep very well there. Where there are no beds yet, one sleeps on mattresses on the floor, but also that is not as bad as it sounds. Altogether you must believe me that life there is absolutely bearable. Of course, the first few days are difficult, until one gets a bit organized, but one gets used to it extremely fast and time passes very fast, for older people mostly by doing nothing. Of course it is terrible for very old people if they are not fit enough and if they have no one to take care of them. They die, accordingly, like flies, but in cases like, for instance, the mother-in-law and the paralyzed sister-in-law of my aunt Annie (your neighbour in Black Fields) one must say they were lucky to be saved. In most of the barracks the washing facilities are wonderful, there are two huge wash-rooms in each floor, with 4 long rows of washbasins and small showers, like in the army. K.'s barracks, for instance, formerly served as a military hospital; there is a small park in the front, washbasins with flow[ing] water in every room and, they say, the most beautiful toilets. These are altogether a separate chapter, according to my view, they are the only thing that is hard to bear in T., forever dirty, water flush never in order, cannot be locked etc., etc. Whether there is heating and they have warm water, as here, I do not know; there was some talk about arranging electric kitchens. Besides, they have an electric washing installation and one can hand in once in a certain timespan one's wash – particularly the big pieces – and one gets them back in 10 to 14 days, beautifully laundered and pressed. I have already written about the food, which is of course very bad, but for money one can buy various things, especially bread, and that is the most important thing. Everyone is working here except for the ill or old people, the types of work are so diverse that I cannot recount them all for you. Like in a veritable city, you can find everything there, starting with the street sweepers – they are called cleaning units – up to the king and his entourage – in Theresian: staff. Artisans, cooks, police, order units, water service, potato pickers and peelers, office personnel, physicians, nurses, etc. There is a postal office in each barrack, and since a visit to the various barracks is impossible without a *laissez passer* (which is difficult to attain), there are special parcel and postal units who deliver letters, food and dirty laundry which the men send to their wives and *vice versa*. Lately, there has been regular visiting and work units, so that the women, for instance, could report to a men's barrack for potato peeling or house cleaning when they wanted to see their relatives. Grandmother lives with Pipsi in one barrack, which, however, is connected with the Hohenelber one without requiring a *laissez passer*. Helen has a certificate with which she can visit her husband daily in order to take care of him. Dr G. works as a physician in the Sudeten barrack and my cousin Fritz Tr. assists him; Julek K. is also a chief physician. Chief physicians and people in leading positions or people who are well versed in a job have usually been, up to our departure, protected from being sent on. We too almost had one foot in Poland in January, but at the last moment, thanks to my position with the post office, I succeeded in extricating us. But these excitements are hard on one's nerves and particularly now it must be horrible in T., as two to three transports leave weekly and it seems to be altogether impossible to extricate one's self. I conclude this from the fact that they write us from there about all the people who have continued their journey. People who had up to now had the best connections. Connections are everything in T., starting with larger food portions up to attaining 'good' jobs. Karl and Grandmother have received all their luggage, but probably all the forbidden things were taken away from them, like from all the others there when the luggage was controlled – like electric hotplates, electric irons, candles, matches, cottonwool, soap, batteries, thermos flasks, preserves, stationery, toothpaste. Foodstuffs have, so far, not been confiscated. True, one hears of the last transports from Prague that some of them arrive completely without luggage. We have also received reports that many lose their luggage on the trip to P[oland]. Thank God, Nori is, according to the last information from beginning of May, still there and works in his field. His household help Sari had to continue the trip and there are reports in B[rno?] that she is very miserable.

We two are doing very well; we have recovered in spite of the work (which is, after all, rather strenuous for Mama); air, sun, food and human treatment have contributed to this and now we could hold on for a few months, if there were not the deep fear of a further trip. We unattached women are in particular danger!! I hope that another transport with labourers will be detached for harvesting and I want to join them again at all costs. I was really not unhappy in T., probably because I was extremely busy there and did not have time to think, but life there caused me not to be able to think at all, I and many other people had the impression that we were becoming totally idiotic, but here, outside, this subsides gradually, one turns slowly into a human being again. Thus it will be ever so much harder to get used to again. I only wanted to wait for the parcel, in order to confirm it. You really overdo it in sending such fine things to me, it was really not necessary. But I was very glad with it and do you know what made me most happy? The little pink box. You should have seen me jump. There was nothing in this world which I wanted so badly, and it was arranged with so much taste. We shall stay here until Saturday 6 June, I shall be very happy, if you want to send us another parcel. But please not do so by express mail. I hurry because there is a good opportunity. You can enclose a sealed letter for K. without worrying. Mama and I send you the heartiest greetings and many thanks!

* * *

Reval
4 May 1943

Dear Cousin,

It is now exactly a year since you heard from me and I am happy to have the opportunity and time to write to you once again. I left

Karl at the beginning of September and I have been here in Estland for the last 8 months. I work as a construction worker in Reval and have become accustomed to the work. We live together with my comerades quite comfortably, rather like in cell 71. The food is unfortunately very inadaquate. I think much of you all and I am very lonely without you. Nori's niece has asked me to send you many warm greetings from Karl; he is relatively all right, he is healthy and in good spirits, as always. But I think he has written to you in the meantime.

I am greatly worried about Alice, have not heard from her for months. I would be very grateful if you could ask her uncle, Rudi Schmidt, Baerckergasse 34, and find out about her. I hope all is as it was with you, I remember with pleasure the fine days we spent together! I would be extremely happy to receive a long letter from you. What do you hear of Pipsi and his family and from all the other acquaintances and friends? All news is highly interesting to me. Please convey my greetings to Nori and to your former neighbour Annie. I would be very grateful if you could send me from time to time a 1-kg package with foodstuff and cigaretttes (for gift purposes). Looking forward to your speedy reply and hoping that you are not angry because of my request. Many many warm greetings,

Your cousin Max

8 June 1943

Dear Cousin,

Your good small parcel arrived just at the right time. You can surely imagine what great joy you have given me. The white bread was particularly wonderful, the filling is wonderful. Your gift for cooking has not changed a bit since I heard from you last time. The day after tomorrow I am starting on my vacation (9 days) and hope to receive a detailed letter from you to my home address. I was quite shattered by what you wrote to me about Karl and his mother and am distressed not to be able to tell you more about him as I left him in the best of moods and health at the beginning of September. I could not imagine in my wildest dreams that he would have to move, his illness and the age of Mama were at that time a total obstacle. I can imagine how desperate you are. As a small consolation I can tell you that the grandmother of my colleague here also moved from there to Ostrov in October and her relatives in Prague receive good news. Besides, I have complete trust in your well-known optimism and courage. I am very sad that there is no news about Alice; the poor thing was so distressed that she had to part from Nori and all her beloved ones, I only hope that she is healthy. Everything else will, hopefully, still be all right. She and her daughter were extremely unlucky, all her luggage was lost during the move. Pipsi is a gifted lad, his parents will have a great help in him. His father was unfortunately very ill when they left. Helen has gone through an unpleasant affair in Th., in which a letter from her sister-in-law apparently played a big role, have you heard anything about this? About myself I can, thank God, report only the best: I am satisfied, all my comrades are young and practical people, they don't get discouraged. We all suffer very much from the separation from our families and are always looking forward to a leave and a happy reunion with them. Please ask your girlfriend to tell Nuri about my letter; unfortunately I do not have time to write home. I would be very grateful if you could send me a big, strong comb, toothpaste and some washing powder. Looking forward to your prompt response and with fondest greetings,

Yours,
Max

P.S.: Nobody of our common friends is here. Small package please to my address in Reval.

My dear Maria,

I do not know how to thank you for your prompt and wonderful fulfilment of my wishes. I am actually embarassed about so much kindness. You have done such a good deed, I worried for the last weeks how I would wash my laundry! It's only a pity that you cannot also send me the Hadyber meadows by special delivery for drying my clothes! Your kind and detailed letter reached me at home, as my leave was extended. You have given me such immense joy with it, I had tears in my eyes when I read about my beloved Hady and all our mutual friends. It is certainly the best solution for you to work with the R. family as housekeeper, even if you surely have much work. You must also have, of course, great trouble providing for all your relatives, but I am convinced that the good God – in whom I still believe firmly, in spite of everything – will reward you soon for all your good deeds and that you will see again all your dear ones, soon and in joy, particularly Spatzerl [little sparrow]. Of course I am very sorry that you have not heard anything about Pipsi and his parents. Unfortunately I must tell you that it was a punishment with Hel. I cannot say more, perhaps later. After my wonderful short leave, I was received here with much joy and now everything continues as before, only my homesickness becomes constantly greater. I have become completely used to the living conditions and everything else is much easier to bear since I received good news from you. Some time ago I had a great and pleasant surprise: quite unexpectedly, I received news from my cousin Hatty, whom you will certainly remember as a good neighbour. He still lives in Pressb and, according to him, Annie is also well! Well, I suspect that you have given him my address, am I right? As to your question: of course we have no vegetables here at all, but I would not have an opportunity to plant any here. On the other hand, I suffer – probably because of lack of vitamines – from an unpleasant rash and would be very grateful if you could send me some talcum. Unfortunately I did not find the tissues and cigarettes in parcel no 1, but you can safely send tobacco and other smoking articles in their original packings, my comrades do it like that. I would be very grateful for tobacco, as my friend is a keen smoker and I would like to do him a favour. I was able to replace the lost things provisionally through a lucky chance and you need not worry therefore. Of course I am worrying about the next winter, but perhaps I'll go on leave again until then. If you have Vermon and saccharine, I would appreciate them too. Please excuse this new list of requests; I know everything is a sacrifice for you these days and please send only what you can really spare. Please, write again as you did, Greetings.

Yours,
Max

* * *

Dear Mrs Maria,

In a hurry – as the opportunity is favourable – I want to tell you a little about Karl. I have seen him since his arrival in T. only once, this was shortly before my mother and I left there for here, where we work in the forest and are satisfied. I found Karl looking really wonderful, better than in B. I could hardly expect to visit him (which is anyhow a difficult matter) and was not disappointed. He is quite his same old self with his optimism and obviously does not feel bad there. He lives with father-in-law and Karlo in one room with about 20 others. As to conditions there, it is a nice bright room, though the air is somewhat stuffy, but one gets used to this. It is lucky that the entire family except for Helen lives in one house, even if they are separated by a courtyard. Pipsi is very competent, works as a carpenter and as such he gets around a lot so that I was

able to see him frequently. Grandmother is also smart and nice, as always. Hedy is a nurse and thus protected from moving on, and her family as well. Karl enjoys a good appetite and enjoys everything, even kohlrabi, which is served every other day. One is weaned very quickly there from being a gourmet; the menu is neither plentiful nor varied. In the morning bitter, black coffee; for lunch soup and a second course, potatoes, cabbage, kohlrabi, twice weekly meat (!) even if it is *à la caballero,* we all like it so much that we have promised ourselves not to eat anything else any more at home!! Utinam – oh, were it only so. You can hardly imagine how much we all want this. We do not talk about anything else any more. Yes, let me continue, in the evening soup, 750 grams of bread for 2 days, now and then a spoonful of jam or margerine. If it is possible, do send something along with people who leave Prague – everything is welcome – with bread and cigarettes you can get hold of anything. For the time being Karl is not at that stage, but we who have spent 6 months there are in a better position to judge this. I hope you have a vague idea who the writer of this letter is, we have met frequently in Swedska Street in the end, when I escorted my master. Karl walks there with a white cane to be on the safe side. Many warm greetings from me and mother.
P.S.: Please send small packet to my old address. Package no. 2 contained: 2 × washing powder, toothpaste, comb and cake. Even the way it is packed is charming! Truly Maria-style.

* * *

Dear Mrs Maria,

I hope you have received my first letter, in which I reported on Karl. Actually, one does not know for sure here whether a letter arrives at its destination or not.

In the meantime a way has been found by which you can also write to me. We are staying here most probably until 7 June, and then we must start on our voyage back – unfortunately not home.

I cannot tell you how hard this is for us, this week we had very bad news from there. I also had 2 postcards from Karl dated 19 and 28 June. On the 19th he wrote that Ribas, Steffi Vrzal and Dornfest continued their journey. On the 28th he wrote that Grossman has been designated for continuation of the trip and that he has volunteered to go along. At the last moment all persons over 67 were excluded. Imagine what these unfortunates have to suffer there, it's like that all the time.

If you want, therefore, to send me something for Karl, I am glad and willing. Please send letters and parcels to Josef Rusicka, Novy Dum c. 33 u Rakownika without mentioning our names. The sign of recognition for me is the sender, Josef Navratil, Brno, Lipska 7. I shall be very glad to hear from you, how you are and everything.

Many warm greetings from Mama and myself,

Yours,
D

Lina sent the letter below from Vienna to Israel in the year 1939. Since it was written on the cover band of a newspaper, it was not opened by the censor. It was given to the Yad Vashem Archive by her son, Mr Haim Rosenfeld.

Dear Robert,

We have received your letter of 11 December on the 17th and would have been glad if there had not been a Misheberach* in the place of [illegible]. The Jew-baiting started again eight days ago, after an

* This is a code word for an unpleasant event.

instigating address by Birk; in the evening nobody dares to go out. The Beit Hamevorach [cemetery] was attacked, all the windows broken, the benches broken, Parochet torn, the Torah scroll torn and thrown out, in the same way everything was demolished in Shool [synagogue], all the Torah scrolls torn on the ground and three were carried away together with the Aron Kodesh [Holy Ark]. The black marble panels on the walls were smashed, and the same in the one of Bojan and Emes ve Shalom; they set fire to Malz-shool [synagogue]. They also set fire to the Great Synagogue. All the [illegible] were also demolished in the Josefson synagogue. We hear the screams of those who are being attacked every night until one o'clock. They visited Eugen Hess this morning and the street looked as though there had been a snow fall: the whole street was covered with feathers thrown out of his apartment. Perhaps Wilson would do something if he heard these things. From where can we expect help to come? From [illegible] two have received old C K, [illegible] has left for Bruenn with his family, leaving everything behind. May the dear G[od] help so that we can report better things soon. Thank God, we all are well. Greetings and kisses

Yours,
Lina

Fritz Brunner has received affidavit from [illegible]
P.S. Am returning from leave just now, am well. Greetings and kiss your father.

Here are two letters written by Lisl Klaus in Prague to Ludia Frankl's daughter, who was married to a German Christian, after Mrs Frankl had been deported to Theresienstadt. From there Mrs Frankl was taken to Treblinka, where she was killed.

Dearest Madam,

I want to respond to your questions now. I am a widow and quite uneducated, from Karlsbad. The household help wanted to write to you; unfortunately I have not asked her for her address, but I know that she was to send another small parcel. I have completely forgotten whether the sweets arrived. Your dear mother took along enough supplies: cake, biscuits, pumpernickel, sausage, meat fat. A carriage is used only for very sick people. Your mother went by tram with a gentleman from the aid committee. Additional friends or acquaintances are not permitted to come along. One does not hear any more about transport no. A AP 516 – according to rumours, all of them are sent to the government old people's home in the Theresienstadt ghetto, which is said to be clean and promises full freedom of movement. My mother, who used to live with me, was recruited on Monday – you can imagine, dear Madam, how I feel. My brother has already spent 7 months in Theresienstadt and, since two transports leave every week, I guess that it will soon be time to say goodbye. Let's hope that we shall meet there?! I am already quite lonely, without friends and relatives. However, I am fully occupied with taking care of the child and the household, and thus the day seems too short for me.

Well, dear Madam, I hope you are a little quieter. There is not much that I can tell you. No one knows for sure the whereabouts of Trude and Georg.

May I hope for further letters?

Very cordially,
Lisl Klaus

* * *

Monday

Dearest Madam,

I am taking the liberty of sending you a few lines. Up to the last minute I was with your dear mother. Leaving Prague was not difficult as all her close friends had been taken away already. I must say, and as a young person I am very surprised, I have never yet seen such quiet and order in winding up of matters here. Unfortunately I have lately seen much leave-taking. Very likely the last hour will also strike for me soon and then I will take your dear mother as an example.

Best greetings
Lisl Klaus,
Prague II

This letter was written on 16–17 March 1943 near Lvov, Poland, in a cinema in which about 600 Jews were imprisoned before they were murdered. One of the policemen guarding the Jews conveyed this letter from a woman to her husband Abraham.

My dear Abraham,

Forgive me for acting so idiotically, without leaving any money. I am sending you something through a person. Abraham and Haiku (Mirku), my dear ones, do not complain – unfortunately fate has willed it like this. I must go the same way as those whom I loved most. I beg of you, take care of my beloved children. Inquire about

Dela (Adele). Whether she is still alive – and kiss her a thousand times from me. Keep well and care for the orphans. I am going to eternal rest.

> Mother *Frieda*.
>
> I have sent 200 zloty via
> B. Come to the gate,
> there you will get the . . .

One of the ways in which signs of life could be transmitted by Jews from the Nazi-occupied territories to their relatives in the free world was the information service provided by the International Red Cross. Here, as an example, is one of those numerous form letters which allowed twenty-five words only; it was sent by the Frydman family of the Warsaw ghetto to their relatives in Palestine.

Polish Red Cross,
Information Office,   July 3 1942
Warsaw,
20 Czerwonego Krzyza St.

APPLICATION
through the German Red Cross, Central Office, Foreign Service
Berlin SW 61, 2 Blucher Square
to the Central Agency for War Prisoners, Geneva
– International Committee of the Red Cross –
for transmitting news.

THE WAR ORGANISATION OF THE BRITISH RED CROSS
AND ORDER OF ST. JOHN — JERUSALEM

To:

Comité International
de la Croix Rouge
Genève

ENQUIRER — WYSYŁAJĄCY — FRAGESTELLER.

Name _ _ _ *FRIEDMAN*
Nazwisko

Christian name
Imię _ _ _ *MENDEL*
Vorname

Address

FEIERBERG 10

TEL-AVIV

Relationship of Enquirer to Addressee
Stosunek pokrewieństwa nadawcy do odbiorcy _ _ _ *ojciec*
Wie ist Fragesteller mit Empfänger verwandt?
Message — Zawiadomienie — Mitteilung.
(Message not to exceed 25 words, family news of strictly personal character).
(Nie więcej niż 25 słow, wiadomości tylko ściśle rodzinne).
(Nicht über 25 Worte, nur persönliche Familiennachrichten).

Drogi Mendlu Chaimie!
Napisz co z Tobą, z Szmulem,
rodzina jego, czy rodzina
Łódzka mieszka u ula.
Jak Twoja córeczka. U nas
wszystko dobrze Czekamy
odpowiedzi.

Date _ _ *2/6/41*
Data

ADDRESSEE — ODBIORCA — EMPFÄNGER

Name _ _ _ *FRIEDMAN*
Christian name
Imię _ _ _ *CHAIM - IZRAEL*
Vorname
Address

MURANOWSKA 12
WARSZAWA

Examples of correspondence transmitted by the Red Cross (and overleaf)

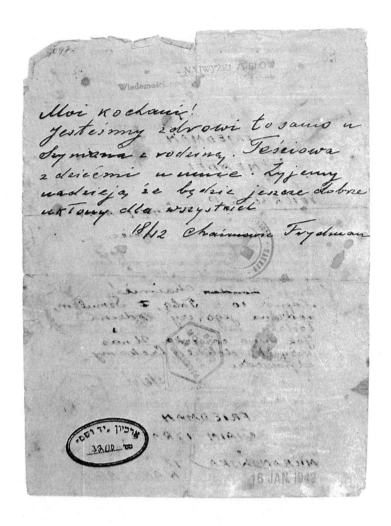

I THE SENDER:	Szmul Wolf Frydman
(First and family name)	
Detailed address:	47 Muranowska St., Apt. 38
	requests to transmit to
2 THE ADDRESSEE:	Mendel Frydman
(First and family name)	
Detailed address:	Palestine, Tel-Aviv, 10 Fajerberg St.

what follows:

(Maximum 25 words)
Dear Parents
We are all well
Heniek is moving from his apartment
How are Benek and family, Reginka and family?
Here without changes
The Hamers are alive the Cukiers [message cut off here]

(DATE) 16.VI.1942

(SIGNATURE)
Sz. Frydman

Marisa (Miriam) was nine years old when her parents, Henia and Shmuel Perlberger of Wielicka in Poland, left her in the care of Christian friends before their deportation to a concentration camp.

The father gave a letter addressed to his relative, Dr Shenkar in the United States, to a friend, Mr Hanula. In this letter the father asks Dr Shenkar to take the child in his care in case her parents do not return. Mr Perlberger did not know the exact address of Dr Shenkar and thus the letter remained in the possession of Mr Hanula.

During the period of the war Miriam stayed with the Christian family, her parents perished and she emigrated to Israel in 1948. There she married and raised a family. The letter reached Mrs Miriam Perlberger-Shmuel in 1981, when she was located by Mr Hanula's daughter, who had been searching for her childhood friend.

Dr Alfred Shenkar and Dr Oscar Shenkar,   25 August 1942
New York,
Factory for chocolate.

Dear Cousins,

I am writing to you at the tragic moment of our deportation. I have
left our daughter Marisa in the care of friends. If we won't be
among the living any more after the war, please take her in your
care! Farewell and do not forget her.

Henia and Shmuel
Perlberger

My dear ones,

I am not able to write at this terrible moment, I am just begging you to find our only child if possible and to take care of her.

Shmuel

Lenka Szpigel of Hungary was deported with her two children, Peter and Jutka, aged about fourteen or fifteen, to concentration camps in Poland and Germany; the mother was separated from her children and lost all contact with them. On scraps of cardboard which she was able to find she wrote during a few days (or, more probably, nights) a long letter destined for her children and made a charm for each of them.

Not knowing where the children were, Lenka never sent off either the letter or the charm; she kept them. The children perished; Lenka survived, emigrated to Israel and married again. After her death, her second husband, Franz Bohm, transmitted to Yad Vashem these items which were so precious to his deceased wife.

My dear Peter and Jutka,

At last I am implementing my wish to write you a letter in the hope that it will reach you. Today, it is the 4th of March, and I am in deep depression, but my patience is of help to me [a few illegible words]. Peter's birthday has passed, neither have we celebrated Jutka's birthday together, and probably we will not be together on mine either. I strongly hope that we will be together again and that we will be able to conduct our life on a new path, with what there will remain for us. Needless to say, I think very much of you and in particular of our separation, which caused me much sorrow and pain. At first I was not able to realize this, but today, looking back, it has become clear to me that it has been a very hard time. I believe and feel that you also are with me in your thoughts, and I hope that with God's help you are well. Thank God, so far, except for a few days, I have been healthy. I have an easy job which I can manage, but I suffer because there is not enough food. Very often, almost every evening, I go to bed with an empty stomach, and then I am all the more worried about you because you are young and it is harder for you to get along with little food. But I repeat that I am sure we will meet soon. During my work I imagine all the time what our reunion will be like and how we will proceed to obtain the things we need. I have many new acquaintances here, among them some whom it will be nice to remember when this is all over, and I hope that this sentiment is mutual. For eight months already we have been going through difficult and sad times. I hope that, in spite of all the difficulties and the hard work, you have kept your health and human image, and I am sure that Jutka, too, has become used to standing on her own feet. I am unable to express the great joy which overcame me when, during my stay in the infirmary, I met a young girl who told me she had been staying in your neighbourhood and also that you were in the same place as Erzsi and little Marika Szenes. About Peter I did not hear anything, but I think that you are together with Bandi. We always talk about you with Aunt Rozsi, Teri and Gunci.

Today it is the 11th of March and I continue to write. I feel even more depressed, because last week, on my birthday, all my life passed before my eyes. In the first place I wish you all the best on your birthdays and I hope that you keep healthy in body and soul, and that you will endure this hard trial, because for our future life we will need both physical and spiritual strength. I hope very much that we will succeed in implementing our plan to reach Palestine and we will try to obtain all the things necessary to equip us for the new life. I do not fear life, I already see that I have enough

ABOVE **Jutka and Peter Szpigel**

BELOW **The 'charms' their mother made for them.**

strength to work, and that everything will turn out all right one way or another. Don't forget to keep strong all the time, trust in God, who has spared us so far and cared for us. We are ever grateful to God. Miraculous things have happened to us – a plane strafed the train in which we were travelling and we remained alive, after all.

Today is Sunday, the 18th of March. Sundays are always more difficult than work days, one is more conscious of the lack of food, especially when one gets 1/3 or 1/4 of the bread ration. One eats less, but perhaps we will withstand this, too, like other things which we have overcome, although we thought that we would not be able to endure them. I do not know whether this letter will reach you, as I so very much wish. But I believe that we will soon be free and meet again. According to the calendar, it will soon be a year since my return from Budapest; so many things have happened since. It is good that you have grown and developed, and your thoughts are surely more mature. I want so much to talk with you, there are so many serious and important matters which I want to share with you only. All the time I think of our relatives and am curious to know what has happened to them, and what has befallen those whom I think are still at home. I think not only of those living but also of the dead. Nobody visits the cemetery. I envy the dead, who are at least spared the sufferings. I often think of grandmother and the aunts, and, if I were to receive news from them, this would calm my worries. When we are together again, we will visit all the family before we leave for Palestine. I am sure that we will manage and that our plans were not made in vain. Do you also think of that plan? I am afraid they will put out the light, so I am ending my letter.

Goodbye
God bless you
Be good and honest

Helene Cohen of Warsaw lost her husband soon after the German invasion. Together with her young son, Izhak ('Jozio'), born in 1939, and her mother, she was sheltered and aided by a Polish woman named Wanda Trebska. Wanda even provided her with forged Aryan papers (her new family name was Kaminska). It is not clear why Helene was arrested and imprisoned in Lublin; her true identity, however, was not discovered. While in prison she managed to send notes to Wanda, presumably through some trustworthy person. From Lublin, Helene was transferred to Auschwitz, still under her Polish identity. She sent four letters from there. After the war, Helene's mother, who had survived with the boy, tried to trace her daughter, but in vain; she had perished. Grandmother and grandson emigrated to Israel.

POSTCARD

Mrs. Wanda Trebska   Lublin
Warsaw-Grochow   12 August
81 Stanislawowska St.,
Apt. 41, Block 10.

Dear Wanda,

We are in the Lublin prison. Please care for Granny and Jozio. Do for them whatever is possible. We are beyond any danger. My only concern is for them. Maybe your father could help them. Tell them not to worry.

Hela

I know your heart, Wandzia, and I count on you.

ON A SCRAP OF PAPER

Dear Wanda,
Help Granny.
For the moment we cannot come.

Hela
Stach

We are alive.

Auschwitz
16 October 1943

Dear Sir,

I inform you that I am well and feel good.

I want to ask you, if this is possible, to send me a parcel. It is permitted to send two parcels a week, 10 kg weight. Bread, onions, garlic, sugar, some fat (butter or pork fat) are preferable. I hope that you will do me this favour, remembering our old acquaintance from Belzyce, and I will be very grateful to you and never forget it.

With kind regards

Helene Kaminska

STAMP IN GERMAN:
Checked

12

K.L. Auschwitz

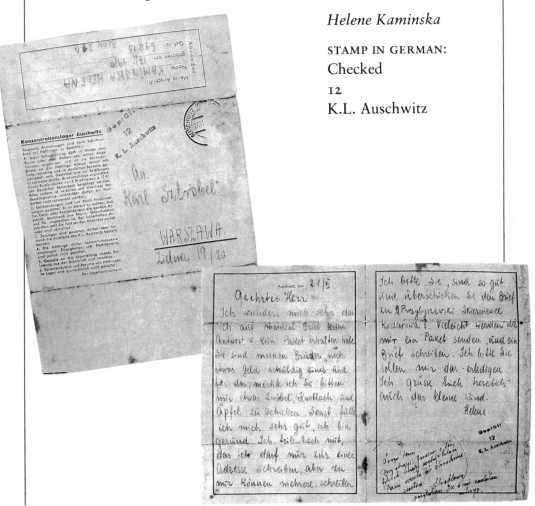

Auschwitz
22 February 1944

My dear ones,

Thank you very much for the congratulations on my birthday.
Thank God, I am still well, I am only longing very much for you
and home. Thanks for the letters and parcels. I am also very glad
that you all are fine and feel good. Do not worry about me. God
helps me, so I am well. I only want to ask you, if possible, to send
me some citric acid or something else sour, because I have an
appetite for this. I am very grateful for everything, and I beg you to
answer me and to send parcels containing less bread, but something
sour. I kiss you.

Your loving
Helene

Please send me some juice.

STAMP IN GERMAN:
Checked
9
KL Auschwitz

Sara and Yehiel Gerlitz of Bedzin, Poland, entrusted their only
daughter, aged six, to a Polish friend by the name of Florczak. With
the presentiment that they would never see their child again, they
left her a letter which she was to open when she came of age.
Fortunately, the parents survived; they were reunited with their
daughter and together emigrated to Israel.

My dear, beloved, little child,

On giving birth to you, my darling, I did not imagine that six and a half years later I would be writing you such a letter. When I last saw you, on your sixth birthday, on 13 December 1943, I had the illusion that I would still be able to see you before my departure, but now I know that this cannot be. I do not want to endanger you. We are leaving on Monday, now it is Friday evening. We are going – Daddy, Pola, and I – with 51 other fellow nationals to an unknown destination. I do not know, my dear child, if I will ever see you again. I take with me from home your picture, which I love so much, I am taking along your lovely chatter, the smell of your innocent, little body, the rhythm of your innocent breathing, your smile, and your tears which my heart, the heart of a mother, could not allay. I take along your last image, as I saw you on 13 December 1943, your prematurely adult look, the sweet taste of your childish kisses, and the hug of your tiny arms. That is what will accompany me on my way. Could it be that Providence will allow me to survive this nightmare and to regain you, my treasure? Should this happen, I will explain to you many things you have not understood so far and which you will probably never be able to understand, since you will be in other surroundings, and brought up in an atmosphere of freedom. My sweetheart! I want you to read this, when, by God's will, you are grown up and mature and able to criticize our behaviour toward you. I desire, my dear and beloved child, that you should not condemn us, that you should love our memory and our entire loathed people from which you originate. It is my desire that you should neither be ashamed of your provenance nor deny it. I want you to know that your father was a person of rare qualities – there are not many like him in the world – and that you can be proud of him. He dedicated his whole life to doing good to other people; may God bless every step of his, protect him, and allow him to regain you! My beloved treasure, you are your father's whole world, his only ambition, his only satisfaction for all his sufferings and pain. Therefore I wish you to keep a good memory of him, if fate should prove unfavourable to us ... I want you to remember your grandfathers and grandmothers, your aunts and uncles – people of great value – and the whole family. Remember us and do not blame us! As for me, your mother – forgive me ... Forgive me, my dear child, for having given birth to you ... I wanted to bear you for our and your pride and joy, and it is not our fault that things took a different course. Thus, I implore you, my one and only darling, don't blame us. Try to be as good as your father and your ancestors. Love your foster parents and their family, who surely will tell you about us. I ask you to appreciate the self-sacrifice of your foster parents and to be their pride, so that they should never

Sara and Yehiel Gerlitz's daughter

have any reason to regret the commitment which they have taken on voluntarily. There is one thing more I want you to know: that your mother was a proud person, despite our enemies' scorn and mistreatment, and, when she was going to die, she did so without moaning and crying, but with a smile of contempt for the enemy on her lips!

I hug and kiss you affectionately; receive all the blessings of my heart.

Your loving Mother

* * *

What can I say to my only child, truly the person dearest to me in the world? One should open one's heart and reveal its inside – no pen is able to describe what goes on in there just now. But I believe firmly that we will all survive and offer our hearts to one another.

Your Father

Naarden [Holland]
15 April 1943

My dear, beloved children,

I hope that this letter will find you in the best of health. I also hope
that you are all earning your living. Dear Mama has already written
to you about everything that you ought to know. We must leave
here now for a camp. We do not know whether we will be sent to
Poland, neither do we know what will happen to us. We confide in
God Almighty that he may save us and keep us alive. It would be
my greatest happiness if I could see you again, my dear children.
But should we – God forbid – be missing after the end of the war,
you will surely inquire about us and try to find out what happened
to us. If we remain alive, naturally we will report to you. I hope
and wish that you should live in happiness and peace, may God
Almighty bless and protect you. My thoughts are always with you.
Now, my dear children, dear Erich, dear Edith, dear Hanna and
dear Simon, may my best and most sincere wishes accompany you.
I remain, sending you my affectionate regards and kisses, your

loving Father and Father-in-Law. May God Almighty hold His protective hand over you.

On 21 January 1943, you, dear Erich, were asked about a certificate to be forwarded by cable. On 7 April 1943 we received the information through the Dutch Red Cross in Amsterdam that the cable was transmitted by the International Red Cross in Geneva to your address. You surely have received it, and we are waiting for the information that the certificate has been despatched. It could be useful to us at this moment, we could perhaps remain in a Dutch camp and not be transported to Germany or Poland. Hopefully, the certificate will still arrive. Let us trust that everything will come out right, after all, with the help of God Almighty. Keep strong, then.

ADDRESSED: Erich Katin,
c/o Goldenrath Nezach,
Tel-Aviv,
Palestine,
3 Israels St.

Edith Fuchs (*née* Katin),
Tel-Aviv,
Palestine,
83 Dizengoff St.

* * *

Naarden [Holland]
15 April 1943

My dear, beloved children,

I hope – should this letter reach you – that you are in the best of health and happiness. Perhaps God will accord us the great luck to see you all again, my sweethearts. Except for the few words which we received through the Red Cross, we have had no detailed news from you for a long time. I hope that you are happy in your fresh marriage. May God Almighty never abandon you and give you joy, good luck, harmony and mutual understanding. May He keep you safe from all evil, protect you and provide you with success and nice incomes in your professions. It is also my desire that you should all live in harmony, peace and friendship. We have been here, in Naarden-Bussum, since September 1940. During the first years after our emigration we stayed with our dear relatives in Rotterdam. About half a year after the war reached the Netherlands, we were evacuated along with many other people. We had the luck to arrive here, where it is very nice, town gardens, meadows, etc., lovely surroundings. One can go to Hilversum on foot, but there are also buses, local trains, etc.; the traffic is vibrant in this beautiful region. Amsterdam is half an hour away by train. In summer there are many visitors here. Last year many of our acquaintances were evacuated from here. We managed to stay on owing to Dad's certificate. By now many people have been sent away to local camps, to Germany or to Poland. We are now, by the 23rd of this month, to be sent to a camp here in Holland, along with many others. This is why I am writing to you. Perhaps this letter will be sent to you after the end of the war by some trustworthy, good people. Perhaps you should make a search for us in case you should hear nothing from us. Be brave and courageous anyway, even if you should receive no news at all. At the beginning we changed apartments several times. Now, for nearly one and a half years, we have been lucky enough to live with fine, good people. For the first time in Holland we had a real home and were feeling marvellous here, were it not for the worry about and longing for our near ones and co-religionists. Here, with our dear fellow tenants, we always found comfort and hope. Now, please note our present address: A.K., c/o Apotheker Elze, Stationslaan 2, Naarden-Bussum, Holland. We have here a small, nice living-room, a bedroom and a kitchen which has been converted from a former bathroom. Now about our near ones: from your parents, Simon darling, I have heard nothing since

Naarden (Holland) d. 15. April 1943.

Meine innigsten geliebten Kinder!

Hoffentlich trifft Euch dieser Brief beim besten Wohlsein an, ebenso hoffe ich, daß Ihr alle Euer Brot verdient. Teil Mama hat Euch alles Wissenswerte geschrieben. Wir müssen nun von hier weg, in ein Kamp. Ob wir nach Polen kommen werden, werden wir nicht und außerdem nicht wahr mit uns geschehen wird. Wir hoffen zum Allmächtigen, daß er uns erlösen wird, und uns am Leben behalten wird. Es wäre unsere Leben behalten wird, es wäre unser größtes Glück, meine lieben Kinder Euch wieder zu sehen. Sollten wir aber nach Beendigung der Kriege, behüte nicht mehr da sein, so werdet Ihr sicherlich nach uns forschen und Du ergründen suchen was mit uns geworden ist.

Wenn wir am Leben bleiben werden wir natürlich selbst melden. Ich hoffe und wünsche, daß Ihr in Glück und Frieden leben möget und der Allmächtige euch behüte. In Gedanken bin stets bei Euch. Nun meine lieben Kinder, lieber Erich l. Edith. l. Mama + l. Simon, meine besten und innigsten Wünsche begleiten Euch. Ich verbleibe mit herzlichsten Grüßen und Küssen Euer Vater und l. Vater und Schwiegervater. Der Allmächtige halte seine schützende Hand über Euch.

Am 21. Januar 1943 ist kein telegraphischer Certificat bei Dir l. Erich angefragt worden. Am 7. März '43. haben wir durch das Niederländische Rote Kreuz Amsterdam Bescheid bekommen, daß das Telegramm dem Internationalen Roten Kreuz in Genf zu keine Adresse l. Erich weiter geleitet wurde. Wir hoffen es sicherlich erhalten und wir warten auf Bescheid. Daß wir das Certificat also in Moment nützen, daß wir in einem holl. Kamp bleiben könnten und nicht nach Deutschland resp. Polen weiter transportiert würden. Hoffentlich kommt noch dasselbe. Wir wollen hoffen, daß uns alles zum Guten und der Allmächtige möge helfen. Bleibt also recht stark.

Erich Katin c/o Goldenrath Nezach - Tel-Aviv, Palestina. Joraelosse 3/04
Edith Fuchs geborene Katin Tel-Aviv (Palestina)
Dizengoffstreet 83. -

---

the outbreak of the war. My dear Anna, your parents have written to us often, they had everything ready for America, but when they arrived in Stuttgart, unfortunately they could only state that the American Consulate was closed down. For some time they still continued to write, but now, for a long while, they have not written. Aunt Martha and Uncle David left Eschwege earlier in December 1941; Aunt Hedwig, Uncle Meyer, Kurt and Louis were sent away from Berlin (where they had been evacuated from Leer) in January 1942. The winter of 1941–42 was particular severe and cold. So far we have received no news from them. Aunt Martha, Uncle David and Granny had been living till then in Eschwege, in the S. and S. Cahn house, where they shared an apartment with Mrs Steinhardt; the Neuhahns lived on the ground floor. Poor Granny had to go through that cruel separation. She then boarded with Neuhahn for some time and she liked it very much there; afterwards she went over to Mrs Loewenstein (Ruth's mother), who had moved to Aunt Paula. Later on, all Jews were ordered to move to the Old People's Home which had been established in the building of the former Jewish school. There, everybody loved our sweet Granny; Mrs Doernberg, the pharmacist, Ruth's mother, etc. – all they wrote about was Granny over and over again, how much they all liked her; but then, she always was so helpful, she knitted and darned for everybody. Meyer Meyberg was there too. I was often able to send her small parcels through acquaintances here whom I helped in their households. Her only joy was when she received some news from us, since she heard nothing from her other near ones. Afterwards, unfortunately, the inmates of the Old People's Home were also taken away, I suppose it was in August or September 1942. They were sent presumably to Theresienstadt in Czechoslovakia. I sent two postcards there, but so far I have got no news. Paula, Erna, etc., Bella L. [and her] parents, etc., have already left, along with Aunt Martha. Shortly before the war Ruth visited us in Rotterdam, accompanied by Lotte. From Rotterdam she travelled to America. Afterwards Lotte was in Amsterdam, as well as Kurt's fiancée, Trude. The latter used to visit us here often; she also left some months ago, and so far we have not had any news from her. Neither have we heard anything from Lotte for a long time. Trude always longed to be together with Kurt at last, such an efficient, magnificent girl! So, my beloved children, now you are more or less informed. I suppose that by now you have received the cable concerning our certificate. I should be very sorry if this causes you expense or trouble. Perhaps this would offer us a chance to stay on here, even if not in the apartment at least in the camp, and not be sent away to another place. May God bring the war to an end soon! In my thoughts I am always with you! I have been writing at twilight and see now, when the light is on, how awfully I have scribbled. Don't be angry with me for this, I do not feel like making another clear copy of the letter. Unfortunately, dear Jo is also staying in the camp, after being imprisoned for some months in Amsterdam. I hope that our other relatives are still here; Chony has a baby, a daughter.

Best wishes and good luck and health to all of you. Let us hope, dear Simon and Hana, that you will see your near ones again; I, too, hope to see you once more, my beloved children.

Love from your devoted
Mother

Below are two letters by Chaim Prinzental of Luck, Poland, written in 1942 to his two children living in Palestine, in Kibbutz Ma'ale Hahamisha.

Today, 3 October [should read September] 1942, it is exactly two weeks since the horrible slaughter in Luck and its surroundings. For two gruesome weeks we – a few Jews who had succeeded in escaping from Luck at the very last moment – have been roaming about without sleeping at night, since death threatens us every moment. Out of the forest and back into the forest. We have become forest men. It happens that for two or even three days we are without a piece of bread, a drop of water. Our eyes are no longer able to shed tears. The heart burns with pain, there is a pressure so strong as to break it, and there is no help. We are all condemned to death. My dear son David – God knows if he is still alive – your mother was like a dove when they led her to the slaughter. I did not witness this with my own eyes; to my great pain and despair fate willed it that I should abandon my dear wife and son and escape alone like a coward. However they are in a better position now than I am, they have already gone through what they had to, and every moment I expect to be caught. I am sitting in a dug-out in the forest where your grandfather used to live and I am writing both of you a farewell letter. Maybe fate will not be so cruel after all and, when the war is over, you will receive it by mail with the help of a goodhearted Gentile.

Thus, I embrace both of you – you and your wife – and I send you my fatherly blessing before my death.

Your unfortunate father,
H.P.

* * *

My dearest children, Jacob and Erna

Another terrible four weeks have passed. Today it is exactly six weeks since the gruesome events in our town Luck and the surroundings. Since then thousands of Jews who had escaped were caught and shot dead. As for me, my bitter fate has preserved me for the time being, so that I may still suffer some time longer. As a matter of fact, Mother and David are the luckiest of our whole family, they have already gone through what they had to, and they surely did not suffer such terrible moral pain as I do, having remained alive. These forty-two days have been awful. Only those who live are scared of death; for the dead it is a salvation. Thus, my children, imagine such a picture: I am sitting in a thick forest and fate willed that it should be exactly the same forest in which Mother was born. An old, gray-haired man squatting on the earth; one would think that I was about seventy; my body is torn and bitten, and I have no shirt on, since I had to throw it away. I did not understand [until now] what a terrible plague the lice were with which Moses punished Pharoah, as is written in the Pentateuch:

'And the wise men could not stand before Pharoah.'* This means simply that the lice were eating them alive. Now I understand it, and it is an awful thing. How happy I would be if I could take a basin of hot water, do some washing, and put on a clean shirt and underwear; and then, may death arrive.

That is that, my dear children. All is lost, but may I at least be the ransom for you, so that you, the survivors, the last spark left of our family, will not be extinguished. I am alone now in my

* Erratic quotation of Exodus 9:11: 'And the magicians could not stand before Moses because of the boils.'

misfortune, my comrade in distress was caught by the murderers on the second day of Rosh Hashana, in full daylight; he had not been cautious enough. They tortured and then shot him. They searched for me, too, they even trod on me in the stack of straw where I was hiding. Yet, for the time being, they have not succeeded. Since then I have been wandering alone at night from village to village, from tent to tent, from forest to forest. But the forest, unfortunately, has started balding, and I also am naked and barefoot, hungry and sleepy. I am walking like a sleepwalker without seeing my own shadow, I am wandering – where to, I myself do not know. Shall I succeed in staying alive? I am not at all sure, it is very improbable. One can still manage somehow, though.

> Goodbye.
> Your unfortunate father,
> *Haim*

A farewell letter from parents to their children in the United States on the eve of their deportation from Bonn in June 1942.

> Bonn
> 12 June 1942

My dearest children,

We are facing the departure into the unknown and, as we do not know how we will fare on this unknown journey, we want to address these few lines to you.

We are deeply indebted to Miss Hella Sente, Bonn, Koblenzstr. 45, so that all of you will be barely able to compensate her for this, in case you don't see us again; also the Erdingen family, who also lives there and whom Eva knew well. I am unable to concentrate, therefore I am brief. I greet and embrace all of you very warmly, your Daddy who loves you so very dearly.

* * *

> Bonn – Enderlich

Beloved, dear children,

I see you so vividly before my eyes. Oh, so often have we hoped that the war would come to an end, then we would have hurried to you, the thought was so wonderful, it kept me going; but unfortunately one cannot evade one's fate. Here, in the icy

Eulenburg [monastery], we are feeling quite well in spite of the horrible food. Unfortunately, we have not allowed to go out lately, fenced in by a large park, this provided sanctuary. Father is, as you know, for the moment still unable to work and thus we had hoped not to leave, to stay here until the end of war and then come to you in a hurry, but fate does not want it.

Miss Hella (Mariechen) Sente was touchingly good to us. Everybody else has left us, but she with her courage and her self-denial gave us strength and help. It was she who helped us again and again with a noble-mindedness, which I am unable to describe. Every Sunday a parcel arrived or she came to visit us together with the Erdingen family (patients of dear [illegible]), the friend of Mariechen and a Lutheran, who were so very good to me. What courage it took to stay in contact with us at that time! May God bless her for the great deed, love and kindness. And you, beloved children, cannot thank them sufficiently. This is my most urgent request, for one cannot describe all this with words. Siblings cannot act like this, so much kindness and noble-mindedness. '*Himmela*' – Heavenly, thus we called the kind one, the one who dared everything in spite of great danger, also the Erdingen family and their dear little daughter. My heart is full of thankfulness.

My dearest ones, she will send you all our things. Yes, I dreamt that I would be able to give you everything personally. Be brave, dearest beloved children, may God bless you, these will be my last words.

Beloved Ruthchen, you are my eldest, you have gone through many a thing in your parents' home – you have such a kind, warm heart, my beautiful, dear Ruth, something strong always emanated from you and I would say to myself: I will ask Ruthchen. I did not need to worry for her, she would think and worry for everyone with us. Utychen, you have gone through hard times in America, you had to work much, my poor Utychen, my heart is full of pain when I think of all of you, but now that Murissa will soon be able to work again, I am not worried any more for your future. Dearest

Murissa, your dear Mother and Guenter have often written to us full of worry and lovingly. In the end they even sent us a sausage with a gentleman who travelled to Germany, it was delicious and two friends called out, God, how happy we are, beloved Murzi. Utychen cares for our ...

Beloved Lily, my Lily, I can see you standing on the stage, how proud I was of my Lilychen. At the moment I cannot write as we are receiving the news just now that we must go with the first transport, I am so headless. Siegmund Meyer could easily let us stay here for 3 months Vanham, Oskar, Ada, Willy are luckier, they can stay on. Klaerchen in Berlin may also stay on, but she has gone so much during the last air raid alarm. At the moment, I can hardly think.

Lilychen, Yupychen, Bobbychen, God, the sweet children, how I would have liked to embrace and kiss you, my heart bleeds. My little Eve, my youngest! What am I to write to you? My darling, be brave. Live your life in health and joy. After all, we have lived our lives, do not feel sorry for us. Always remember how happy I would be to know that you are happy. I have a last wish, beloved children, keep firmly together, whatever might happen, love each other dearly, then you will live the way I want it. Little Eve always gave me her last penny. How beautiful it was in Hohenzollernstr., when we were waiting for Uty-Murzi in the summer. When Lilychen and Jueppchen surprised us. Jueppchen was always so good and did not help with words but with deeds. And all your sacrifice with the visa, Lilychen, Eve, Murissa, Jueppchen, thousand thanks. Lily dear, one of the violins is very fine, I am giving it to Bobby, it is an Italian violin.

Beloved Eve, I hope you will soon find a dear man whom you will love, dear girl, then you will have your own home, your child and then you will be happy. Don't be so choosy, you only have to love him. God, if I could only see him, look into his eyes and quietly whisper into his ear: Make my Eve happy! Beloved children, fondest thanks for all your love. Each one of you separately has made me so happy with your love, I was after all so little and so proud of my blond beautiful children. Thus I am taking leave of you. I embrace you with tears and kisses. All loving God protect them and make them happy – don't cry now because of our Jewish fate. It is not fate – it is real VIOLENCE and with what GREATNESS it is being carried out. The Buchners are arriving now. From up here the transports go into the universe.

Utchen, Hildchen, beloved Ben, Evchen, I wanted to write much more to you, but I am not able to any more. Ing. Meyer was after all not able to keep us here any more, as he had assured me at the time. Poor humanity – no, it is indiscribable, you dear ones! Thank you a thousand times for all your great love – Gertchen, become a great man. Evchen, if I could only look at you now. God bless you all. Also Archen, Editchen, fond kisses – Ruth, Lily, Evy, Murissa, Jueppchen, Bobbychen . . .

Thus in three months time no Jew may be in Germany any more.

Emil Woehl wrote the letters below in the period between 20 June 1941 and 7 November 1942 in the city of Hradec Kralove, Czechoslovakia – a legacy for his son Yeshayahu (Heinu).

---

20 June 1941

My dearest boy,

Slowly the fear settles in my mind that we won't see each other again and thus I want to tell you something and hope that what I am writing down now will reach you one day. I don't think I need assure you, first of all, that I think of you constantly, but perhaps you think at times that I did not do everything in order to join you, although you have asked me to do so after Mother's death. And therefore I must – I have the urgent need – to explain myself to you. True I could have been more energetic in the application for a certificate. But perhaps you know how unpleasant and difficult this was. Not only would I have had to seek the protection of influential persons, I would have had actually been forced to use my elbows and perhaps also intrigues. You know that I was unfortunately not in the Zionist organization until the year 1938, for reasons which are not dishonourable. I have fulfilled all the normal duties of a Zionist, probably more than most of the organized ones, however I was not ready yet to dedicate my entire life to this aim, which means to study *Iwrit* [Hebrew] diligently, to acquaint myself with the culture of a people and possibly to emigrate to Eretz Israel, thereby foregoing great material advantages, as it seemed at the time. Most of all, I was not yet ready to take on such a responsibility for the two of you, for your mother and for you. In the year 1938 I already knew that I would not suggest any other alternative to you and I am convinced that you also are satisfied with this decision of mine. I know you have a hard life ahead of you. However, if you survive the war, you will be able to live a life which will be free of all consideration for hostile surroundings, as we always had to do. I hope that later on you will live a natural healthy life with our people, even if you miss many of the so-called amenities of bourgeois life.

I have lost my thread a little. That I did not see to it to get a certificate – probably I would have had to fight for it – I do not know how, and you will understand this. On the contrary, I believe you would also have been opposed to such behaviour. But there was a second opportunity to join you which I neglected to take advantage of. Even more so. I was registered for the last illegal transport ship and I withdrew my registration. I did not think it would work. Not that I was afraid of the hardships. But I could not believe that the boat would really reach its destination. And even though I know that most of the people are in Mauritius and some, a few hundred of them, have perished in the explosion on board ship, I still regret my decision. Perhaps we would have seen each other never the less; and, if the country which is our last hope is really lost to us, I would have liked to be there during that honourable defeat. On the other hand, I am not sure – who knows himself really, after all – whether the basic cause was not simply indolence. It is already difficult to start a completely new life, and it is difficult to oppose good friends who warn you about undertaking a dangerous step. But it is useless to worry about this, I only want to make sure that you do not condemn me.

I can explain more easily how I left Vienna. I could not have predicted that the remains of the school I was directing would get into trouble after my departure because of the incompetence of my two successors. Three months later the school was actually closed and I would not have a real field of activity in Vienna today. Here I merely have the satisfaction that my siblings are glad to have me here, although I cannot be for them, especially not Aunt Ella, what I would like to be and what they perhaps expected from me. I have nothing to do here; I keep myself busy somehow, but it does not give me the feeling that I work. I have enough time to study Hebrew, but it is very hard for me. Apparently I am already too old. But in the country I think I would learn it quickly enough in order to know sufficient to do some very modest, preferably manual job. Physically I feel healthier than some years ago. I am not at all attracted to intellectual work, like teaching, in Eretz Israel because I would always feel unable to perform such a task perfectly. After all, I have lived my life mainly based on wrong principles. I would only want to earn my living through the labour of my hands.

But you must not think that I am unhappy or sad here. I do not think of the future very much, have made it my guiding rule to treat the present bad times as a transition and intend to bear philosophically any change in our situation caused by external factors. You know, I have always been lucky with people, people like me and that strengthens my will to live and also a little my self-esteem. Even if I do not quite agree with other people in their estimation of me, I guess their judgment is not quite mistaken. I enjoy working in the garden, my physical fitness, the letters of my former pupils, the company of my friends, but also a good book, although not quite as much as formerly. I often sit here, at Eav's desk, looking at two pictures which hang on the wall, namely Mother's picture from the time when she was a young girl (the pencil drawing by E. Ascher, the brother of Mrs Zdenni Cohn from Ramat Gan), and your picture, next to the birch tree in [illegible], and I think about past times; but I enjoy even more imagining your present life and I would like to have reason to hope that you will have a good, happy future ahead of you.

* * *

2 January 1942

My dear boy,

I fear that you are deeply worried about our fate at the moment. Unfortunately there actually is reason for this concern. Up to date nothing has happened to us; however, we must take into account that we too will be evacuated. The turn has now come too for the provincial communities, probably Pilsen and Budweis first. When our turn comes, I do not think we all will go at the same time. Anyhow I cannot imagine that they would also deport Uncle Max. According to the information from Theresienstadt – and it seems that this is only probable – women and men live separately and that would be almost impossible for Uncle Max. But, for the time being, nothing has happened. During my waking hours at night, I think about you a lot. I am glad I receive the Hradec Kralove news, though it is naturally only very little. How I would like to know more about your actual life. How many decisions you have had to take already without being able to consult me. Who are your friends? How do you feel about your superiors and co-workers? What are your feelings towards the country as such? Are you in an organization? Have you found friends, perhaps a girl friend? How can you stand the physical work? And all the things which Mother would want to know were she still alive, whether you are interested in making yourself smart after work, whether you are well taken care at Mrs S.'s, how you spend your leasure time, if you have a chance to listen to music, etc. I don't suppose you ever have a chance to play the piano. And Mother would, most of all, long for a little picture of you. Up to now Mother has not missed anything by not being with us any longer. She would suffer extremely. You will remember that she was unhappy when she saw a careworn face on the bus. We once went to a very good film, I don't remember now which one, and Spanish refugee children who were sent to England and were disembarking were shown in the newsreel. There were some very sad faces among them. Mother could not forget this all through the evening; after a few weeks she hardly remembered the actual film, but had to think constantly about these poor children. How she would have suffered now. From all sides only sad news, messages about death and misery. How she would have suffered with Aunt Annerl. Poor Heinz is no longer alive. Unfortunately he never understood me, nor was I able to convince him that Jewish youth and Jewish people must together finally realize the situation and dedicate their power toward Jewish matters. It is a great pity that he died, he was a particularly decent and intelligent human being. He had a permit to go to England in August 1939, but did not use it because he wanted first to arrange for his parents to get a reference from the bank where he had been employed and it did not come through in time. But many others have fallen on unhappy times without even a semblance of guilt. How many have been deported to Poland, to Lodz (Lietzmannstadt) and Theresienstadt these days, and how miserable they are there. There are many deaths. Sometimes I think one will never again be able to be happy; on the other hand, I feel as I did during the First World War, when I was frequently ashamed of the fact that I did not endure any real hardship. As long as I was in Vienna I could still do something for the poor and unfortunate. As a whole it was nothing, but the individuals were very grateful. Here I have no field of activity. I wrote about this before in my last letter.

When I think about the far distant future, I think first of all about the future of our people. And here I do not think about the many people who consider themselves as belonging to us by chance, but of those who identify enthusiastically with the Jewish people, of you in the country who are ready to make sacrifices and of the renaissance of Jewish culture. I am really sorry that I did not go about things the right way earlier, when I had the opportunity. I had many friends in the Bar-Kochba organization in Prague as a student, during that great time when Hugo Bergmann, Viktor Keller, Robert Weltsch, Jugo and Leo Neumann and Friedl's uncle, Alfred Kraus, lived there. Perhaps it was too hard for me to dedicate myself entirely to the Zionist idea. Anyhow, I have subsequently lived a life, in my profession, which is half lost these days. Well, it does not help today to worry about this. The external life of a human being is often directed by chance. And I can be only grateful for such chances. Chance brought me to Vienna, where I met Mother and where you were born. And, after all, that was happiness enough. Sometimes I feel that you have inherited from me quite a burden of inhibitions, which have deprived me only too often of happiness in life. I would like to know if your new life has changed you.

For the time being I am keeping these letters in my suitcase. If I have to leave, I shall send them to Aunt Muschi, who is really a good friend of ours and who would certainly take good care of them.

The day after tomorrow is your birthday. You will come of age. I hope that you have ahead of you a fine life, perhaps I will be fortunate to enjoy a little of it with you.

My dear boy, farewell.

With the aid of a Dutch woman, Cilli Dzialowski of Holland sent this farewell letter to her four children, who resided in England during the war. Her son Hy survived in a hide-out in Holland. The letter was transmitted to Yad Vashem by one of Cilli's daughters, Mrs Jakobovitz, who now lives in Canada.

Enschede, Holland

1 April 1943

Beloved, precious children,

In these final moments, before I join your dearest father, and will, like him, lose my freedom, there is an urgent compulsion within me to tell you the following.

You are in our thoughts by day and night; our love for you makes our life even under these present difficult circumstances worth living; we long for the moment when we shall once more be able to embrace you with outstretched arms – *you*, our most precious possessions – and we have faith in the future, that this supreme joy will be granted us.

'Beloved Sparrows' – I must call you this once more, as I used to do when you were still very young – should circumstances alter course for us and we, according to the will of the Almighty, not meet again, I beg each one of you with all my heart to lead honest and straightforward lives *always*, and to support one another whenever necessary. Your young and only sister will receive your utmost thoughtfulness and love. And Hy, your eldest brother, who has missed you no less than ourselves all these years and who has suffered greatly through agony and fear, must also be close to your hearts. Unfortunately, uprooted as we have been here in Holland, we were never able to give him the secure parental home atmosphere for which he longed so much. Many times the longing for you and the desire to be reunited with you were so overpowering and strong in us, as well as in him, that we feared we could bear it no longer.

I know what a treasure we have in you, my beloved ones, and that you are committed and firm and of strong character, that – *Baruch Hashem* – you are all blessed with that essence of personality which makes you liked by your fellow men and will surely find favour in the eyes of the Creator. This knowledge brings me consolation. *Never* deviate from the path of God-fearing behaviour and always be guided by the example of your beloved father. Our constant thoughts of you have accompanied you so far on your road through life, and our blessings will never leave you!

This letter will reach you through the efforts of a fine Dutch lady who was always wonderful to us and constantly gave us courage for the future, which we accepted gratefully.

My Precious Children – I bless each one of you from the distance with the traditional blessing, also in Daddy's name: 'May you be happy and successful in life; cling one to the other; and *never* stray even one step from the path, from the precepts of our TORAH.'

I embrace and kiss you and now feel truly united with you,

Always yours,
Mummy

Otto Weidt, a half-blind German, was director of a workshop for the blind in Berlin. During the war years, his workshop became a refuge for many Jews, as employment there gave them a chance to survive. Some of his workers were prominent personalities. When the Jewish workers were deported to concentration camps, Weidt maintained contact with them and wrote them letters to keep up their spirits.

For his brave achievements, Otto Weidt was honoured by Yad Vashem with the title of one 'Righteous Among the Nations'.

Out of the large collection of letters from his deported Jewish workers (which he transmitted later to Yad Vashem), one postcard is published here; it was written by four of 'his' Jews while being transported, as they say, to 'the labour camp Birkenau, post office Neu-Berun'. They dropped the postcard during the journey, as can be deduced from the request to the finder to forward it.

No such place as Neu-Berun ever existed; the deportees were probably given this fictitious address intentionally by the German authorities in order to suppress the ill-famed Auschwitz, of which Birkenau – a name far less known then – was an extension.

16 May 1944

Dear Colleagues,

For 24 hours now I have been travelling to the new labour camp, Birkenau, post office Neu-Berun. Stop sending any parcels immediately and send information, as you have done so far, to the above address. We hope that work will be finished soon and expect with joy to see you again in good health. We are in the best of spirits and all of us are well. News from you will reach us there as well, we are waiting impatiently for mail from Mrs Zimmermann in

Der Berghof   Popp

particular. No need whatsoever to worry, you can rely on us. Thousand greetings – Alex, Georg, Kathe. Greetings – Else.

ADDRESSED TO: The Personnel of the Weidt Workshop for the Blind
                 Berlin, 39 Rosentaler St.

POST SEAL: Pudlau, Oderberg, Upper Silesia

ON THE REVERSE
SIDE OF THE CARD:

The finder is asked to drop this card into the letter box. Many thanks!

INSTEAD OF A
POSTAGE STAMP,
THE AUTHOR WROTE:
Postage plus fine will be paid by the receiver.

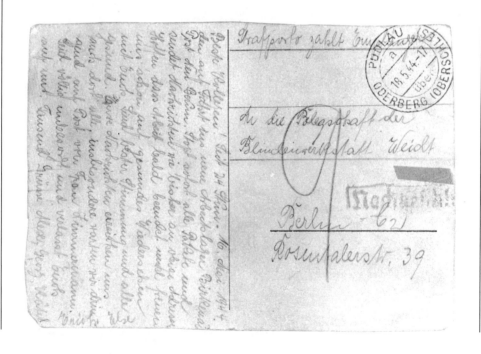

Beloved Stefanie,

Forgive me, remember me with love. There was no choice. My
life was beautiful to the end, in your love and in the friendship of
those who surrounded me with loving care. I thank you, each one
of you separately, you who have supported me in these days of
spiritual torment. I hope to die in peace with the world and in the

hope of grace and love. Be strong. Maybe one day justice and humaneness will build up a new life. Support each other. I am becoming drowsy, my pulse weakens. I am happy and am falling asleep. My life is completed and was beautiful. I am without bitterness.

Anton Schmid was a German Wehrmacht sergeant sentenced to death for saving Jews and executed by the Nazis. Yad Vashem recognized him posthumously as a 'Righteous Among The Nations' and planted a tree in his name in the Avenue of the Righteous at Yad Vashem, the Holocaust Martyrs and Heroes Memorial, Jersualem. Below are Anton's farewell letter to his wife and a letter from an army priest concerning his execution.

Office,
Field post office no. 12546 A,
III.
Concerning Sergeant Anton Schmid
Criminal matter

O.U. 25 March 1942

Mrs Steffani Schmid,
Vienna XX,
Klosterneuburger street 78.

Referring to your letter of 16 March 1942, this is to inform you that a law suit is being conducted against your husband at the local military field law court. Since the case is not yet concluded, no further information can be given to you at this point.

Captain and commander.

Vilna

13 April 1942

My dear Steffi,

Thinking of you in joy and in sorrow, I am informing you, my
dearest, that my verdict has been announced today and that I must
part from this world, am sentenced to death. Please remain strong
and trust in our dear God who decides the fate of each one of us.
I could not change anything any more, otherwise I would have
spared you and Gerta all this. Please forgive me, therefore, I did
not want to cause you this pain, but unfortunately it cannot be
changed any more. I am ready to die since this is the will of God
and His will be done. You must resign yourself to this. I ask you
again, please forget the pain which I inflicted upon you, my dear
ones, and keep quiet about it. After all, I have only saved human
beings, even if they were Jews, and this was my death. Just as I
have always done everything for other people, I have also sacrificed
everything for other people. Everything else you will hear, because
a comrade will visit you and he will tell you how the court judges.
Please do read the letters 1–4 which you are sure to receive, you
will understand from them that I had intended it differently, but I
considered you, my dear ones.

My dear ones, I beg of you again, please forget me, it had to be
this way, fate has willed it like that. I am concluding these last lines
which I am still writing to you and I send many greetings and kisses
to the two of you and to you my dearest one in this world and in
the other world where I shall be soon in God's hand and I remain
your ever loving

Toni

* * *

Dear Mrs Schmid,

I am herewith fulfilling the sad duty in transmitting to you the last lines which your dear husband has written. On Monday 13 April he had to say goodbye to this world. I was with him during the last hours in order to give him pastoral support. He received once more the holy sacraments and strengthened himself in prayer and in God's word and remained strong to the last moment. His last words were the Lord's Prayer, which I prayed together with him. His last request and his last wish was that you also should remain strong and that you should comfort yourself. I join in this wish, hoping that you find comfort and that there will be a meeting in God and that you continue your hard path in life in strength and courage and in confidence in God's providence.

Your dear husband's grave is in the soldiers' cemetery 1914–1918, in the Wilna part of the city Antotol.

With the most devoted greetings,
Fritz Kropp
War Priest

Samuel Potasznik was a member of the underground in Brussels. With two other companions, he was given the assignment to kill a high-ranking Gestapo official. They carried out the mission, and the Nazi authorities set a price of $\frac{1}{2}$ million Francs on their heads. The three of them were arrested on 9 September 1943 and executed in the prison. The text published here is Potasznik's farewell letter to his wife.

Brussels
8 September 1943

My dear Doll,

These are the last words which I will write to you, since tomorrow morning, at dawn, I am to be shot. I am sad that I was unable to see either you or the children again before my death. But there is nothing that can be done about it. I must accept this. My dear Doll, my last moments are entirely devoted to you and the children. I ask your forgiveness for having left you without any support and protection in life. Still, in these last moments, I implore you once more to pardon me and not to bear a grudge against me for this. You know very well that I was unable to act otherwise. And I implore you to devote a good thought to me from time to time. You will explain to the children, when they are of age, why I had to die, so that they may understand.

I am also asking you to forgive me if I have hurt you. Believe me, my Darling, I have had a hard life, my character was formed in bad conditions. You will understand that it was not out of spite that I made you suffer. Don't think too badly of me, my dear, and forgive me all the harm which I have possibly caused you. Then I will die peacefully, being sure that you have forgiven me. I have suffered much since my arrest and I hope that I have redeemed by my sufferings all the faults which I might have committed. I beg you not to allow the memory of their father to be erased from the minds of our children; then I could be sure that I would not be dead entirely.

A curious coincidence: I am going to die on our little Daniel's birthday. So in future you will be able to commemorate, on 9 September, a double anniversary. In this way my little boy will be able to continue my life without interruption.

I know that it will be very difficult for you to manage with two children. I have shed many tears for this reason, but that's that, it is too late, I can do nothing about it. It would be the dream of my life to be able to exist and to work for you. But fate has decided otherwise, so I must give in. I hope that our friends will not abandon you, and you can surely count on the devotion of Mr and Mrs Bartholemus. I have taken into account the possibility that our little son might be adopted. You can decide about this at the proper time.

My beloved darling, my heart breaks when I think that I shall never see you again, but my despair is in vain; there is nothing that can be done about this.

As to our children's upbringing, I would ask you to see to it that they grow to become simple, balanced children who will love nature and outdoor life. I don't think that it is essential to make Daniel study, except if he shows exceptional talents, and if your material conditions will permit this. Otherwise I prefer him to be a good, specialized worker. As to our little daughter, I can't say anything, as I do not even know her. How cruel it is and how much I suffer, my darling, that I must depart without even knowing my own child.

Immediately after the end of the war it will be necessary for you to get in touch with my parents, with Guta and Halek, to convey to them the news and perhaps to consider together the way in which you could arrange your life.

My beloved darling, from the depth of my heart I wish you to be happy. You deserve this because you are good and affectionate.

I only ask you once more to care for our children, to direct and advise them. Hence, do not allow them to separate from you until they are grown up and able to lead a life of their own.

I implore you again, my beloved Doll, to forgive me for all the harm which I have caused you by leaving you in such a difficult situation. Don't bear me a grudge, dear, since you know the reasons which have directed me. I return again to [the upbringing of] our children, dear beloved, teach them to live a simple life without much useless noise, a life amid nature, and teach them to love beauty. Actually I have realized that one of my greatest faults was that I wanted everything at once. Work, studies and all the rest of it. You must decide together when the children reach the age of 15–16 which profession they should choose. Don't go beyond your material possibilities. If you cannot afford to let them study, it would be better that they should learn a profession. It is necessary that the children have sufficient free time. If you could teach them gardening, this would be an excellent pastime. During this last period, before the condemnation, I actually dreamed about a little house in the country, with a big garden where one could grow vegetables and flowers. I am sure that you would have loved it. But now, everything is finished. Still, you could perhaps implement this project alone. For me, it's too late. I did not know how to live. I devoted too much effort to things which were not worthwhile. Do you understand, my beloved, what I mean by this?

When I review, in my memory, our life together, I find beautiful moments, but also bad ones. Anyway, I can assure you that I have always loved you from the depth of my heart. Maybe I did not always know how to reveal this to you, which I should have done. You know very well that this is a fault of my character. Please pardon me for this, now when the hour of my death is approaching, I implore you, my beloved, and please think above all of the happy times we have spent together. The hours pass slowly and the moment of death draws near. Now, I cannot cry any more. I think of death with courage and the only thought that worries me is that I am leaving the three of you in so unfortunate a situation. It is hard to die in such circumstances, especially when one has small children, whom one would wish to bring up with love and devotion. But fate has decided otherwise and I cannot help it. I probably have not merited the joy to be a father to my children.

Beloved darling, it is you who must be both their father and mother. Again: bring them up so that they may be persons of value and be happy, this is my only worry and my only wish. Your photograph as well as that of the children is before me and I will die with your dear images imprinted on my memory. After the war, if you wish to have details about my last days, you can turn to the following address: Mr Victor Moraux, 24 Grande Place, Marienbourg.

My beloved darling, the hour approaches and I must prepare myself to accept death with courage and serenity. It is no use troubling my mind with all these questions, as I actually cannot change anything. The deed will be done, this is Fate's verdict and nobody can escape it. And it is exactly at the moment when new life is beginning to sprout that I must leave this world. My dear, I thank you wholeheartedly for the good hours which I was able to enjoy owing to you. They were the only ones in my life of work and studies which were really happy ones. Believe me that my heart is breaking at the thought of being separated forever from you and the children. But I cannot indulge in weakness, I must be brave. So you will be able to tell the children later that their father died bravely, and that his death should be their guide in life. My beloved darling, the children's happiness lies in your hands and I know that I can trust you. Lead them cleverly, show them the way they should follow, be their comrade and friend, so that they may be able to confide to you all their joys and all their pains. Direct them on the path of honest and clean work, the one which I too have followed, and when they are of an age to understand, tell them about my efforts to be a man, to acquire more wisdom and to develop a sense of beauty.

The future of the children is in your hands. This is a great responsibility, but I know that you will fulfill it perfectly; I trust you, my beloved darling.

Be happy, all three of you; be happy, my beloved darling, be blessed for all that you have done for me. If this is possible, say goodbye to my parents for me, and to all my brothers and sisters, as well as to all my friends.

Goodbye, my love, I kiss you tenderly for the last time,

Sam

26 October 1942

My dear, good Mamotschka!

I thank you so much for all your care, the books and parcels with
which I nourish myself. The potato purée was still quite warm
when I got it, so that after such a long time I had for once warm
food again. I cannot bear the food here. Be so kind as to send me
my small panties and a towel *frotté*. Please, no more books by John
Knittel, I have read all of them. Maybe Vera [Vena?] could be so
kind as to lend me one of her small Tauchnitz volumes of Bernard
Shaw. If so, I would also need my English–German dictionary (it
is on the piano or on the desk). [Follows a line cancelled by the
authoress or the censor] so that I sometimes am quite desperate.
You cannot imagine how much I regret having done that stupid
thing which now causes so much distress to you, Remus, and me.
Please, Mamico, take good care of yourself and your health, I am
very worried that something might happen to you because of your
being upset. You must be healthy in order to help me and the baby
afterwards. Without you I am lost. I am thinking of you day and
night, and I long for you very much. Give Remus my greetings and
tell him that he must, as far as possible, fight with the doctors for

his foot, and by no means agree of his own will to an amputation. Should it not heal, there will be time enough to do it a few years later. By now I have already been away from home for four weeks and a few days. It seems years to me. I think that since Montreux I have never wept so much, even though I know that this is stupid and only harms the nerves, but I am hardly able to control myself. Answer me immediately, my only beloved Mamotschka. Don't worry about making mistakes in German. Please give my regards to my friends and acquaintances who are helping you by providing things for me. Pray for me, the poor heathen (as you used to call me).

I embrace you and send you a thousand kisses, my dearest and best one, and I remain your always loving, although not always obedient,

Liana

* * *

19 January 1943

My only one, beloved Mamotschka!

I would like to fall on my knees before you and beg you to forgive me for the awful pain that I have caused you. Of all my sins, this is the gravest one before God, and I pray to Him every day to pardon me for this. You have sacrificed everything for me and done all that was possible. Yesterday I said goodbye to Remus forever. I think I need not tell you anything more, since you surely felt what was going on in my heart these last days. I promised Remus to do whatever is possible to give life to our child, whom we love before it is born, and, if it is a boy, to name him Arno-Alexander. He should be christened Alexander in the Russian Church. Mamico, I beg, I implore you, keep strong and live for my child, do not abandon my child. Love it as you loved me, you will have more joy from it than from me. In the name of God and Jesus Christ who commanded eternal love and reconciliation, I ask you to forgive me and to pray for me as I do for you every hour. My belief in God and His eternal love and mercy is strong and unshakable. I recommend my child to the loving hearts of Vena [Vera?] and Mrs Eugenie, Ina and Sergej. Give my regards to my friends and ask them not to forget me. Please send ne one of your icons. Please ask Father Sergej to visit me, perhaps they will permit this. I have here with me a passport photograph of you; you know, the last one which you had made. It is a great consolation and some kind of refuge for me. Still, I hope that we will see one another again. I think of you, I dream of you, I love you madly. Mamotschka, my darling, I know that you love me and that you forgive me. I embrace and kiss you a thousand times, my good *Koschka* [pussycat] – Mama.

> Always your –
> *Lanuschka.*

* * *

Directorate of the
Women's Penitentiary Prison

Berlin NO 18,
10 Bernim St.
4 May 1943

On 12 April 1943, Liana Berkowitz gave birth to a female child in this institution.

In charge:
[Signature] *Kuhn*, the Matron

Attestation to be presented to the office for Ration Cards.

Heil Hitler!
In charge:
ILLEGIBLE SIGNATURE

* * *

Schutzpolizei,
Head of the Berlin-Treptow District,
Berlin,
47/48 Graetz St.
29 June 1945

I attest herewith that the copy on the reverse side is identical with
the original.

Head of Police District No. 231
In charge:
ILLEGIBLE SIGNATURE

* * *

Copy

The Military Prosecutor General   Berlin-Charlottenburg 5
[Oberreichskriegsanwalt]   4–10 Witzleben St.
StPL (RKA) III 525/42   20 May 1943

Mrs Margarete Rehmer
Berlin-Neukolln
33 Harzer St.

```
Der Oberreichskriegsanwalt          Berlin-Charlottenb.5,den 20.5.43
   StPL (RKA) III 525/42             Witzlebenstr. 4-10
                                     Fernruf: 30 06 81

   An
      Frau Margarete  R e h m e r
            in Berlin - Neukölln,
                  Harzerstr. 33
   Anlage: 1 Brief

         Das gegen Ihren Sohn Friedrich Rehmer durch das Reichskriegs-
      gericht am 18.1.1943 verhängte Todesurteil ist am 13.5.1943 voll-
      streckt worden.
         In der Anlage erhalten Sie einen Brief, den Ihr Sohn noch
      an Sie geschrieben hat, zugesandt.

                                     Im Auftrage
            F.d.R.              gez. Dr.  R o e d e r
            gez.Unterschrift
      Heeresjustizinspektor.
```

Encl.: 1 letter

On 13 May 1943 your son, Friedrich Rehmer, was executed in
implementation of the death sentence passed upon him by the
General Court Martial on 18 January 1943.

Enclosed please find a letter which your son had written to you
previously.

In charge:
SIGNED Dr Roeder

Identity of the copy
testified by
SIGNATURE
Heeresjustizinspektor

Women's Penitentiary Prison,
Berlin NO 18,
10 Bernim St.
16 June 1943

My dear, good Mamotschka!

I have received your letter dated the 7th, as well as the things which
they finally handed over to me last week, and I thank you from the
depth of my heart. I am very sorry that my last letter worried you,
but you must understand that I am sitting here without any mental
occupation and without reading anything sensible, and on top of
this the death of Remus and Irka's bad health. Things now have
improved somewhat insofar as I received two good books through
the high school teacher on Saturday. A real Pentecost joy. Irka,
too, is better now, thank God. She receives rice cereal with glucose
every three hours and really has put on weight, but last Tuesday
at 2 o'clock it seemed that her end was near. Her face was quite
blue already, ice-cold, with immobile and glassy eyes. We naturally
caused a big alarm, and a real panic broke out. I was quite crazy
with fear and I shouted and cried. My sentence seemed to me child's
play when compared to that fright. A few days after you receive
this letter, please come to fetch Irka, because she must now leave
here. But take her on a day when the Office for Ration Cards is
open, since you will immediately need both the food and clothing
cards, without which you can get neither a bottle nor a nipple. Best
bring Aunt Elli with you when you come for Irka; for you alone it
will be too tiresome. Please arrange for a good pediatrician as well,
it will be necessary to have one at hand – so the local doctor told
me – as the child is very fragile and needs particularly good care.
Dear Mama, do not send me food any more; even though the Court
might give its permission for this ten times, I do not receive these
parcels, and I do not want strange, indifferent persons to profit
from products which you save for me from your rations. I was

forced to let them be used by the institution, because part of them was already rotten, and I did not want to burden the M.K.G. [meaning unclear] with a return mailing. I have just learned that my sentence was confirmed on 18 April and thus is valid. Only now the preparation of the appeals for clemency starts, so there is still some hope. Hopefully, before my separation from Irka, I will still be able to watch her getting better. I embrace and kiss you a thousand times, my beloved Mamico –

Your *Lanka*

P.S. If possible, let me know on which day you will take Irka. The best hours are between 11 and 12.

Pray for me, I am awfully miserable.

* * *

Berlin-
Plotzensee,
7 Konigsdamm.
5 August 1943

My only, dearest, beloved Mamotschka!

This is the end. Today, at dark, your Lanka will no longer be alive. My consolation and hope is my little Irka who, thank God, has no notion of what is happening around her. Mamico, you were to me the best mother on earth. You have done for me whatever it was possible to do, and I thank you. Forgive me my death, forgive me every offence which you have suffered from me, every ugly word; I beg you, I implore you, crown your work as a mother and keep strong!!! You must remain healthy and alive, you must live for my

Irka who lies in her cradle, a full orphan. Protect her, care for her, live for her. Owing to you, I go to my death with the strong conviction that my darling is in good care. You must fulfill the last wish of your dying child. Bring Irka up to become a clever, energetic person, make her learn as much as possible. Teach her to believe firmly in God and His eternal love, mercy and justice. She shall love and honor the memory of her parents. Have her baptized in the Greek Orthodox church. Keep for her my hairlock and photograph, the letters from Remus, my books and personal effects. Divide my clothes between Vera [Vena?] and Gerda, give my best regards and kisses to Mrs Rehmer. Ask her to care well for Irka, this was also the last wish of her son, which she can read in his last letter to me. To Uncle Milja, Ina Senescha, Aunt Lena, Vera [Vena?], Aunt Jenny and all, all my friends give my last and best regards and the request to care for Irka, should she be in need. I believe in God, in eternal life, and that we will see one another again. In the next world, I will pray for you and Irotschka, and protect you. I am calm and self-controlled and not scared of death. All the possessions to which I am entitled according to Henny

Berkowitz's will I leave to Ira with the request that you should dispose of them. Moreover, I appoint you – as well as Mrs Rehmer and Dr Dmitri Jewsiejenko, if something should happen to you – to be Ira's guardians. The last months and particularly the period after my separation from Ira were unbearable to me and – on the one hand – I am glad now that these torments will soon come to an end. God has shown me great favours. He has let me experience everything that a woman can experience: He has given me a child. At least, I have been – although not for long – a mother, and this is the most beautiful thing on earth. Once more, Mamico, be strong, be courageous, love your child and live for Irka. Now I will direct my thoughts and senses toward God and prepare myself for my route to Christ, trusting in His love and mercy. I make the Holy Sign of the Cross on you and Ira. Take Ira to your home once the danger of air raids is over, so that she may have a home and a childhood as beautiful as mine has been. I kiss and hug my Irka and her sweet little hands and feet. I embrace and kiss and greet you for the last time; I kiss your hands and accept your blessing. Your calm, unfortunate,

Lanka

German Red Cross,
Kurmark Hospital
Eberswalde/Mark,
3 September 1943

Mrs Katharina Wassiljews-Berkowitz,
Berlin W 30,
3 Viktoria-Luise Square.

In accordance with your telephone conversation with our nurse in charge of Ward No. 16, we ask you for an advance payment of 40 marks for your grandchild Irene Berkowitz, who was admitted here on 25 August 1943.

Deutsches Rotes Kreuz
Krankenhaus
Kurmark

Eberswalde/Mark, 3.9.43.
Telefon 3065
Postscheckkonto: Berlin 199669
Girokonto Nr. 47, Stadtsparkasse Eberswalde

An Frau
Katharina Wassiljews-Berkowitz

B e r l i n W 30
Viktoria Luise Platz 3.

Wir beziehen uns auf Ihr Telefongespräch mit unserer Stations-schwester von Station 16 und bitten um eine Anzahlung von Rm.40.—für Ihr am 25.8.43 hier aufgenommenes Enkelkind Irene B e r k o w i t z.

Heil Hitler!
I.A.

Deutsches Rotes Kreuz
Krankenhaus Kurmark
Eberswalde/Mark

56062 C 1727

These are the Jews who have worked in Kulmhof (Chelmno) between Kolo and Dabie in the death camp:

1 Herszkowicz, Josef of Kutno
2 Plocker, Mojsze of Kutno
3 Plocker, Fajwel of Kutno
4 Szlamowicz, Szyje of Grabow near Lodz

5 Radkiewicz, Nojech-Wolf of Lodz
6 Charach, Chaskel of Leczyca
7 Wachtel, Simche of Leczyca
8 Wachtel, Jisroel-Chaim of Leczyca
9 Jastrzebski, Beniek of Leczyca
10 Nusbojm, Aron of Sanniki
11 Sztrasburg, Ojser of Lutomiersk
12 Sztajer, Gecl of Turek

These are the last Jews who worked for the Gestapo in Chelmno, which is situated between Dabie and Kolo. These are the last days of our lives so we give a signal maybe there still will be relatives or acquaintances of these persons. So you shall know all Jews who were sent away from Litzmannstadt were killed in a very cruel manner they were tortured and burnt goodbye if you survive you must take revenge.

This note is written by people who will live for only a few more hours. The person who will read this note will hardly be able to believe that this is true. Still, this is the tragic truth, since in this place your brothers and sisters stayed, and they, too, died the same death! The name of this locality is Kolo. At a distance of 12 km from this town [Chelmno] there is a 'slaughterhouse' for human beings. We have worked here as craftsmen, because among them [the Jews who were brought here] there were tailors, leather-stitchers, cobblers. There were 17 craftsmen there [illegible word], I can give you their names.

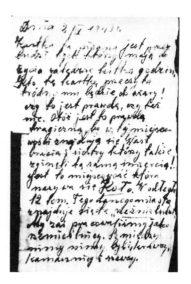

1 Pinkus Grun of Wloclawek
2 Jonas Lew of Brzeziny
3 Szama Ika of Brzeziny
4 Zemach Szumiraj of Wloclawek
5 Jeszyp Majer of Kalisz
6 Wachtel Symcha of Leczyca
7 Wachtel Srulek of Leczyca
8 Beniek Jastrzebski of Leczyca
9 Nusbaum Aron of Skepe
10 Ojser Strasburg of Lutomiersk
11 Mosiek Plocker of Kutno
12 Felek Plocker of Kutno
13 Josef Herszkowicz of Kutno
14 Chaskel Zerach of Leczyca
15 Wolf Judkiewicz of Lodz
16 Szyja Szlamowicz of Kalisz
17 Gecel of Turek.

These are, then, the persons' names which I give here.

These are only a few people from among the hundreds of thousands who died here!

In 1980 a farewell note written in Greek was found at the site of crematorium No. 3 in Birkenau (Auschwitz). Yad Vashem received a copy of it from the Auschwitz Museum. The note, which seems to be incomplete, was probably written by one of the members of the Jewish *Sonderkommando* who worked there.

To my dear ones

Dimitrios Athanasios Stephanidis, Ilias Cohen, Georgios Gunaris and all my close friends, Smaru Eframidu of Athens and other friends whom I will always remember, and finally to my beloved fatherland, Greece, whose faithful citizen I always have been.

I left Athens on 2 April 1944 after going through torture for months in the Haidari concentration camp, where all the time I received packages from the good-hearted Sfaru, and all that she tried to do for me remains in my memory forever in these terrible days which I am now experiencing.

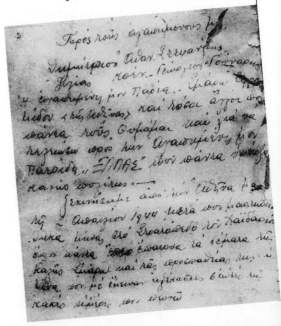

The original of this document was in the possession of the Jewish Museum which existed in Vilna for a few years after the end of the war. The museum was closed by order of the Soviet authorities. Recently Yad Vashem received a copy of the following document.

A Request to My Jewish Brothers and Sisters

Dear sisters and brothers,

We are asking a big favour of you: In the first place forgive us all the wrong that we have done to you, maybe in deed, maybe in word. We do not understand for what we have been punished so heavily. They take our lives, but never mind their taking our lives, but our children were tortured devilishly, for example eight-year-old girls were taken for sexual intercourse with men. These little girls were ordered to take the male organ into the mouth and to suck it like a mother's breast and those discharges which men spill the girls were forced to swallow and they were told to imagine that this is honey or milk. Or they took a girl aged twelve, tied her to a stool and until 5 Germans and 6 Lithuanians had each had sexual intercourse with her twice she was not untied and released, and the mother was forced to watch over her child that she should not cry. And then they took the mothers and stripped them to the skin, put them against the wall with their hands raised and tied and plucked all their hair to the flesh and told them to put out their tongue, pricked it with pins and then everybody came and pissed into [their mouths] and smeared their eyes with shit.

Woe is me! And they told the men to take out their members and then stabbed these with glowing wires, and held on until the wire was black and said You have lived long enough you yids, *zhydas*, we will slaughter all of you. It is not enough to kill but they must be tortured so that they should not want to live and see Stalin. They

Kochane moje siostry i bracia zwracam do was z ... prośbą, najpierw darujcie żeśmy wszystko ... tego zrobili może uczynili może powiedzieli ... co na nas taka wielka Kara spadła że ... życie ... rają, ale że życie zabierają to nic ale nasze ... sposób męczeń. na przykład 8 lat dziewczyną były brane do stosunków płciowych męskich kazano ... dziewczynek małych brać interes płciowy do ust jako pierś ... kazano połykać i mówiono wyobraźcie ... albo mleko. Albo brano dziewczynkę lat 12 ... do taboretka i za nim 6 mężów 5 ... stosunki płciowe Każdy po 2 razy to ... puszczał a matka musiała stać i patrzeć ... dziecko żeby to dziecko ... krzyczało. A ... matkę rozbierają do naga ... przywiązują ... do gołego ciała a ... szpilkami a potem ... a guznem oczy ...

Oj a dla mężczyzn kazano powybierać swoje płciowe interesa i napalonemi drutami wbijali do środka trzymali za nim drut z czarnej i mówiono dość życia judu żydas wszystkich wykatrupim zabić to nie sztuka ale trzeba wymęczyć żeby im nie chciało się żyć i stalina robać. Brali nam palce odkrajali na ręku i na nogach i nie można było zawiązać tak krew z ... przez cztery dni nas męczyli drżący Każdy dzień jednakowo a potem do aut na Ponary to nas było 45 osób w jednej wywrójce ale mieliśmy połączenie z drugą grupą tunelem tam było 67 osób dorosłych i dzieci i mieliśmy tylko komunikacja z jedną polką która nazywała się Marysia wdowa Marysia miała troje dzieci. Ta Kobieta brała od nas ubrania męskie damskie futra męskie futra jedwabna bielizna wszystko mieliśmy to ona ... i nam dostarczyła żywność. A potem ... my się wzbogacili ona zdobyła iż na ... świata 40 tys. i 50. 60 tys. marek seized our fingers and toes and cut them off and did not allow us to dress [the wounds] so blood soaked through for four days. So they tortured and tormented us every day the same way and then on to cars and to Ponary and we were 45 in one hide-out, but we had contact with another group through a tunnel: there were 67 people, grown-ups and children. And we had contact only with one Polish woman, whose name was Marysia, a widow; Marysia had three children. That woman took from us men's clothing, women's furs, men's furs, silk underwear – we had everything – so she took and supplied us with food. And then, once we had made her rich, she got money – 40,000 [zlotys] and 50–60,000 marks – so she would go to Szyrwin and bring 3 or 4 pigs, 2 poods of pork fat, 5 quintals of wheat flour, 20 kilograms of butter, eggs, all this our property for our money. She gave the Germans booze and brought [the food] by car from Szyrwin and told us to give her 5 kg of gold – if not, I will betray you to the German Gestapo – and gave us a time limit. We did not manage to hand it over to her so we sent a Jewess eight years old to Marysia that she may extend the time limit and wait, but the child did not come back. She [Marysia] took what we had sent her – golden watches, rings, brooches and other things – and the girl was killed and burnt, and two days later the Lithuanians and Germans found us and tortured and tormented us for 5 days as was described and they they took us to Ponary. This letter I am dropping on the way to Ponary for good people that they may give it to the Jews when there will be laws again that they should kill at least one person for us 112 persons and they will have a great merit for their people. With tears in our eyes we ask for revenge, revenge. I am writing in Polish because if somebody finds a letter in Yiddish he will burn it but if in Polish and a good and generous person will read it and hand it over to the Jewish police, that they may do something to that cruel cruel woman who shed on herself and her children so much blood, we beg. 30 children of ours perished, so may at least 3 of hers perish, 2 boys and 1 girl, and she with them.

Dear brothers, we all implore you with tears, don't forgive that hag. We don't know her family name. Her first name is Marysia, a widow, she has three little children, 2 boys, 1 girl, lives in Wielka Pohulanka No. 34 in the courtyard on the left. Everybody knows she is a smuggler [Her apartment is] near the Church of Jesus' Heart, the superintendent [of her building is] Rynkiewicz. We say goodbye to you. Goodbye to the whole world. We call for revenge.

This is being written
by *Gorwicz* and *Ass*

Both testaments published here were found on the terrain of the former ghetto of Shavli (Siauliai) in Lithuania. They were written on the eve of the final liquidation of the ghetto.

---

11 July 1944

Document!!!

On leaving the ghetto and taking a step between life and death, I left behind me a few photos of my nearest ones in the hope that somebody would find them while digging and searching in the earth, and that this person would be so kind as to transmit them to one of my relatives or friends in America or Palestine, if there will still be any of them left. My name is Frieda Niselevitch, born in Vaiguva.

To my dear and esteemed father, Nahum Zvi Niselevitch, my sister, Shoshana Stein, her husband, Miha-Yehuda Stein, and other relatives in Kelme who have remained alive; to my dear niece, Esterl Stein, in Zhagare. I embrace affectionately my dear ones who will receive this document, may they know that I have remained alive so far, the only one of the family, about the others I do not know anything. My dear Mamele I saw for the last time in prison, of my brothers Simhe [and] Aizik Meir Niselevitch they were in Ponevezh before the war.

I send my greetings to my Jewish brothers who have remained after the Inquisition, may they be devoted sons to our fatherland, the Holy Eretz Israel.

Frieda

Siauliai

Document

We attest that on 7 July 1944 the order for the evacuation of the ghetto of *Shavli* was issued.

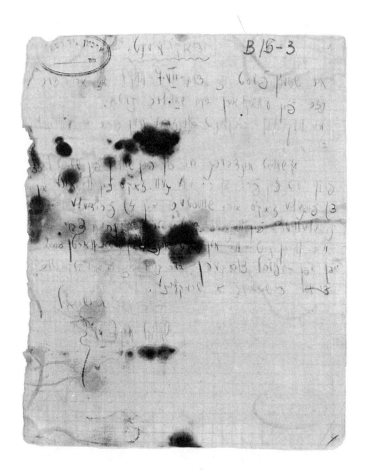

We want our names to be known for the generations to come: (1) Shmuel Minzberg, son of Shimon of the city of Lodz (Poland); (2) his wife Reizele née Saks of Vaiguva; (3) Feigele Saks, the latter's sister; and (4) Friedele Niselevitch of Vaiguva, Nahum Zvi's daughter.

We do not know to what destination they are sending us. In the ghetto 2,000 Jews are waiting for the order to leave. Our fate is unknown. Our state of mind is awful.

> May the Kingdom of Israel
> arrive soon, in our days.
> *Shmuel Minzberg*